WHAT ARE THEY SAYING ABOUT
FUNDAMENTALISMS?

What Are They Saying About Fundamentalisms?

Peter A. Huff

PAULIST PRESS
New York/Mahwah, NJ

Library of Congress Cataloging-in-Publication Data

Huff, Peter A.
    What are they saying about fundamentalisms? / Peter A. Huff.
        p.   cm.
    ISBN-13: 978-0-8091-4357-3 (alk. paper)
    1. Religious fundamentalism. I. Title.
BL238.H84 2008
200.9′04—dc22

                                                                    2007024146

Published by Paulist Press
997 Macarthur Boulevard
Mahwah, New Jersey 07430

www.paulistpress.com

Printed and bound in the
United States of America

Contents

To

Darwin A. Caldwell

In the end we are always rewarded for our good will, our patience, fairmindedness, and gentleness with what is strange; gradually, it sheds its veil and turns out to be a new and indescribable beauty.

Friedrich Nietzsche, *The Gay Science*

What we need…is respect for the beliefs of others and the readiness to look for truth in what strikes us as strange or foreign; for such truth concerns us and can correct us and lead us farther along the path. What we need is the willingness to look behind the alien appearances and look for the deeper truth hidden there.

Joseph Ratzinger, *Many Religions—One Covenant*

Acknowledgments

The assistance and wisdom of many people have contributed immensely to this book. My students at the University of Puget Sound, Saint Anselm College, and Centenary College of Louisiana tested many of these ideas in the laboratory of classroom discussion. My colleagues at Centenary College, especially Susan Brayford and Sam Shepherd, have offered helpful advice and constructive criticism. A summer research grant from Saint Anselm College helped to initiate the project. Without the foresight of the T. L. James family, who generously funded Centenary College's endowed chair in religious studies, this sort of project would be virtually impossible.

I am also grateful to Natasha Wilson, my talented summer research assistant, and to the excellent staff at Centenary's Magale Library. My editors at Paulist Press deserve profound appreciation as well. Kathleen Walsh enthusiastically supported the project when it was barely more than a proposal. Christopher Bellitto, author and scholar in his own right, provided the balance of patience and prodding that every writer needs. I wish to thank the University of the South's School of Theology for permission to use material previously published in the *Sewanee Theological Review*. I also wish to thank Routledge (Taylor and Francis Group, Ltd.) for permission to use material previously published in the *Encyclopedia of Fundamentalism*. As always, I am deeply indebted to my wife Mary and son Malcolm for their encouragement and understanding. Mary's keen editorial eye has saved me many times from turgid prose and infelicities of style. I take full responsibility for any errors of fact or interpretation.

This book is written out of the twin convictions that fundamentalism is one of the most important forces in contemporary religion and that the study of fundamentalism is one of the most exciting fields in the discipline of religious studies today. Nobel laureate Albert Schweitzer once described the modern period as "a dangerous medley of civilization and barbarism." Those whom the media and the academy have dubbed "fundamentalists" are well aware of the disturbing nature of that unstable combination. Despite their disagreements over a host of ultimate things, they agree on one crucial point: our historical moment is somehow frightfully out of joint—filled with contradictions and cataclysmic potential. This book, written in a time of terrorist rage and superpower revenge, is for all who would peer into the *coincidentia oppositorum* that defines the mystery of our age.

Introduction

The rise and apparent triumph of fundamentalism surprised even the most astute of the twentieth century's culture watchers. Now we recognize fundamentalism as an enormously important development in modern experience. For controversial Baptist leader and Moral Majority founder Jerry Falwell, fundamentalism was "the religious phenomenon of the twentieth century."[1] Scholars across the academic spectrum have agreed, calling it "one of the defining elements of the religious mosaic" of our era and "one of the most significant political phenomena of our time."[2] At present, fundamentalism energizes millions of people in their religious commitments, identities, and aspirations. It is a potent shaping factor in every branch of the 2-billion-member Christian family. According to some observers, it offers a reliable glimpse of Christianity's global future.[3]

Fundamentalism also serves as a transforming force in virtually every major religious tradition on the planet. Since the Iranian Revolution of 1979, Islamic fundamentalism has made such a tremendous impact on the world scene that no one can afford to ignore it. The terrorist attacks of September 11, 2001, drove that fact home with brutal clarity. Other global fundamentalisms, too, are dramatically reordering once familiar patterns of power and allegiance into unpredictable networks of ambition, revenge, and sacred rage. Fundamentalism in all its varieties could well be the most significant religious movement of the twenty-first century. Future generations may look back on our age and call it the age of fundamentalism.

Despite fundamentalism's imposing presence on the contemporary religious landscape, it is one of the least understood movements around. Much confusion surrounds the phenomenon. The term itself is one of the most contested in contemporary usage. The English word *fundamentalism* was coined in 1920 to self-define a conservative party within U.S. Protestant denominations opposed to what was then known as the higher criticism of the Bible. Today the term *fundamentalism* is applied, often indiscriminately, to a wide variety of cases in a broad spectrum of contexts. Renegade Mormon polygamists in the Great American Desert and fugitive Taliban warriors in the mountain hideaways of the Pakistani-Afghan border are described as fundamentalists. So are middle-class Pentecostals and home-schooling Opus Dei Catholics in the suburban enclaves of secular America. Fundamentalism is so amorphous a concept—and so heavily freighted with ill will—that some specialists in religious studies have dropped it entirely from their lexicon. Recognizing the "politics of nomenclature," as one historian put it, they maintain that more is risked than gained in its continued use as a formal category.[4] What may be one of the English tongue's most versatile terms of insult, they insist, deserves no place in either the civil classroom or the scholarly monograph.

For the majority of scholars who maintain that *fundamentalism* can be utilized with integrity, the term means different things. Some scholars—especially historical theologians and historians of American religion—limit the term exclusively to a certain type of antimodernism found among disenfranchised North American Protestants during the first decades of the twentieth century and to the varieties of conservative evangelicalism fostered by that antimodernism. Generally, mainstream biblical scholars use the term to describe a particular method of scriptural interpretation or hermeneutics out of step with contemporary historical-critical approaches to the Bible. Academic systematic theologians, when they do not ignore it altogether, view fundamentalism as a fossilized form of grassroots orthodoxy scratching out a meager existence in the "corners of cultural life, sterile and ineffective," as Paul Tillich once said.[5]

Still other scholars—most often social scientists or specialists in the field of the history of religions—detach *fundamentalism* from its original American Protestant milieu. They employ the category as a technical term signifying neo-traditionalist and restorationist movements restructuring major religions around the world. Scores of studies argue for the existence of Catholic, Jewish, and Islamic fundamentalisms parallel to the original Protestant prototype. Many claim to find evidence for fundamentalist strains in Hindusim, Buddhism, Sikhism, and other non-Abrahamic Asian traditions. For these scholars, the concept of fundamentalism exposes "family resemblances" that unite religious protest movements across the globe. Most serious scholars of the international phenomenon agree that fundamentalism has something to do with an oppositional stance toward at least selected elements of modernity or postmodernity. The growing trend in academic circles is to employ the term in a purely descriptive fashion. It is also becoming increasingly common to use the awkward but accurate plural form of the term: *fundamentalisms*.

In some quarters, though, *fundamentalism* is still a highly charged term of derision—a convenient label used in a pejorative fashion to dismiss, condemn, or demonize realities judged to be deviant forms of true religion. Public figures outside the academic community—most notably journalists, politicians, and clergy—continue to use the term uncritically as a catchall for all sorts of illiberal and reactionary impulses in contemporary society. According to the American mass media, forces ranging from international terrorism to local school board squabbles animating the U.S. culture wars may all be classed as examples of fundamentalism. Ever since journalist H. L. Mencken tied the fundamentalists of the 1925 antievolution *Scopes* trial to the problem of bigotry in America, fundamentalism has been associated with intellectual obscurantism and lowbrow literalism. For almost as long, it has been linked with fanaticism, violence, and what historian Richard Hofstadter once called the "paranoid style" in politics.[6] These images are so firmly fixed in the public mind that antifundamentalism may be the last legitimate form of religious intolerance in contemporary society.

Despite the disparate uses of the term and its profound limitations, *fundamentalism* is now a permanent fixture in public discourse and an indispensable category in theological and religious studies. Since the 1970s, the interdisciplinary study of fundamentalism has emerged as a respected academic enterprise whose relevance is recognized far beyond the research institute and university classroom. Though the international field remains a cottage industry still partially ghettoized in the broader academy, it has met with a remarkable measure of success—especially, as historian Bruce Lawrence has noted, in its efforts to move fundamentalism "from front-page horror stories to fruitful academic analyses."[7]

Plan of the Book

This book attempts to answer the call for a brief, comprehensive, and balanced introduction to major trends in the academic study of fundamentalism. Like other books in this series, it is intended to meet the needs of the advanced undergraduate and the beginning graduate student or seminarian as well as those of the general educated reader. While the book is written with readers from a variety of religious and cultural backgrounds in mind, it is primarily designed for an audience approaching the subject from the perspectives of the diverse community of American Christianity. As a beginner's guide to the rapidly expanding interdisciplinary field of fundamentalism studies, the book provides a critical survey of the ways in which anthropologists, historians, sociologists, theologians, political scientists, and religious studies scholars have attempted to come to terms with the origins, development, nature, and varieties of fundamentalism.

The six chapters of the book address key areas of the academic enterprise. Each provides descriptive analysis of the work of scholars who have made significant contributions to the international field. The first two chapters introduce the reader to the quest for the historical origins of Protestant fundamentalism in U.S. culture. Popular stereotypes, reinforced by decades of anti-fundamentalist propaganda, have routinely portrayed early fundamentalists as benighted rural southerners. These chapters survey attempts to reconstruct the actual conditions that made it possible for fundamentalism to come into being. They lead us into a dense network of innovative institutions that provided the initial infrastructure for fundamentalism and acquaint us with a loose confederation of creative individuals who can be described as the fathers of fundamentalism. They also introduce us to the new breed of scholars in the early twentieth century who first recognized in fundamentalism an intriguing religious phenomenon worthy of serious academic attention.

The third chapter raises the issue of methodology in fundamentalism studies. While the first scholars to submit fundamentalism to critical scrutiny were university and divinity school theologians, the scholars who established fundamentalism studies as a distinct field of academic inquiry in the 1970s and 1980s were largely professional historians. Since that time, scholars from many different disciplines have contributed to the growing body of research on the subject. Their procedures vary as much as their motivations and disciplinary assumptions. Today literary criticism, ethnographic field study, psychosocial research, philosophical analysis, and autobiographical introspection complement traditional historical and theological methods.

The fourth chapter moves away from paradigmatic Protestant fundamentalism and reviews controversial attempts to transfer the category of fundamentalism from the economy of North American evangelicalism to the world of modern international Catholicism. It explores the antimodernist impulse in recent Catholic thought as well as the fascinating Catholic underground of conspiracy theories, supernatural intrigue, and countercultural political activism.

The final two chapters travel far beyond the world of Christian fundamentalisms. They guide the reader through the ever-expanding scholarly literature on the varieties of global fundamentalist experience, examining the works of pioneering researchers who view fundamentalism as a mythic vision or worldview capable of finding a niche in nearly any religious tradition. According to these scholars, the forces of Jewish separatism, Zionist radicalism, Hindu nationalism, Buddhist patriotism, and the multinational Islamic resurgence—in conjunction with the varieties of Christian fundamentalisms—constitute nothing less than an axis of sacred rebellion in the modern world.

Perspectives

For decades, most writers on fundamentalism have been non-fundamentalists, ex-fundamentalists, or antifundamentalists. In the chapters that follow, we will see many examples of the first two categories. Little space will be devoted to antifundamentalist literature. Nor will we encounter very many fundamentalist writers. Though there are significant exceptions to the rule, few fundamentalists have contributed significantly to the project of fundamentalism studies. Fundamentalist intellectual culture has not fostered the sort of critical mentality necessary for what would amount to self-study. Fundamentalists find themselves at odds with many of the ideas and values informing the modern academy's "culture of inquiry."[8] The suspension of judgment, a hallmark of mainstream intellectual life, is regarded by many fundamentalists with great suspicion. Consideration of multiple points of view is also judged to be problematic. The school of thought called phenomenology, especially influential in setting standards for contemporary academic religious studies, requires a strategic bracketing of the researcher's own beliefs and prejudices — what some have called methodological agnosticism. Fundamentalist purists see this requirement as tantamount to apostasy. With some justification, they see the relativism implied in historical consciousness as inimical to religious certainty. For the fundamentalist, certainty always trumps academic reputation.

To be fair, we should also acknowledge that many fundamentalists are simply too busy to study themselves. Driven by a sense of divine urgency to propagate and defend what they perceive to be the truth, while simultaneously resisting what they consider to be the new intolerant orthodoxies of secularism and scientism, they simply do not have the leisure to indulge in the critical study of their own movements or ideologies.

Fairness also requires that I reveal something of my own background and approach. As a product of America's evangelical subculture, I am intimately acquainted with certain forms of Protestant fundamentalism. I was raised in the Southern Baptist community — the denomination that Samuel S. Hill, dean of southern religious history, once called "a marvel, a wonder, a spectacle, a mighty force."[9] About half of my postsecondary education took place in the Southern Baptist Convention's extensive university and seminary system. The "fundamentalist takeover" or conservative resurgence that began to transform these institutions in the late 1970s and 1980s overshadowed much of my undergraduate and seminary experience.[10] The remainder of my training occurred in a state university religious studies graduate program and a doctoral program in historical theology at a Jesuit university. Long attracted to its sacramental ethos, mystical sensibilities, countercultural social witness, and classical theological style, I eventually entered the Catholic Church during graduate school. I would describe my present spiritual orientation as an inclusive religious humanism at home in the broad context of ecumenical Catholic Christianity.

To date, my work in fundamentalism studies has been dominated by an effort to change the way the international interfaith dialogue community looks at fundamentalism. Since the 1999 Parliament of the World's Religions in Cape Town, South Africa, I have endeavored to expand the pluralist paradigm currently governing interreligious dialogue to make room for a recognition of fundamentalism informed by an empathetic appreciation of universal human religious experience. Pluralism was a great achievement of twentieth-century philosophy of religion. It granted many mainstream Western Christians the moral and intellectual warrants necessary to abandon the exclusivism of traditional Christian doctrine. Ironically, however, many advocates of interfaith harmony who endorse pluralism intentionally or unintentionally limit the scope of their pluralism. For them the vision that imagines many paths to the sacred excludes at least one: the contemporary phenomenon known as fundamentalism.

Pluralism's premier philosopher John Hick, a former fundamentalist himself, has spoken of fundamentalism as a psychologically stunted, ethically inferior form of religion on the edge of an "intellectual twilight zone."[11] Harold Coward, another prominent proponent of pluralism, has gone even further, calling fundamentalism "the opposite of true religion."[12] One suspects that pluralism's verdict on fundamentalism stems from a theological criterion alien to the logic of pluralism itself. I also get the impression that many participants in dialogue see opposition to fundamentalism as one of the unifying factors among themselves.

From my perspective, fundamentalism does not represent a distortion of genuine religion—a dwarfed or twisted creed—but rather one distinctively modern way of being religious among others. A demythologized fundamentalism may even possess a hidden wisdom that nonfundamentalists could appreciate and selectively appropriate. The Catholic-evangelical dialogue has already reinvigorated a stagnant Christian ecumenical movement. The new Mormon-evangelical dialogue holds similar promise for intra-Christian understanding. Beyond that, as I suggested at the 2004 Parliament of the World's Religions in Barcelona, fundamentalism represents the final frontier for the wider ecumenism of interfaith work. Opening dialogue to the phenomenon of fundamentalism, I believe, will revolutionize ventures in interreligious harmony.[13]

Defining Evangelicalism

Finally, preliminary definitions are in order. Since three chapters of this book deal with Protestant fundamentalism, we need a working definition of *evangelicalism,* the host religious culture for fundamentalism. Evangelicalism's significance for this book is its function as a context for the development of original Christian fundamentalism. Just as evangelicalism is a special type of Protestantism, fundamentalism is a special type of evangelicalism.

One shopworn definition of an evangelical is "anyone who likes Billy Graham."[14] Since Billy Graham has been so inherently likeable, and since he is beginning to be eclipsed in popular awareness by less charismatic would-be successors, this definition no longer communicates exactly what it was intended to say. It is also inadequate because nonevangelical forms of religion, at least in the United States, have been so effectively evangelicalized in recent decades. Many American Catholics, for example, understand their own tradition in terms largely borrowed from the ethos of U.S. evangelical Protestantism. If liking, or thinking like, Billy Graham constitutes the criterion for evangelical identity, then it would not be too far-fetched to suggest that virtually every religious American is an evangelical of one sort or another. This state of affairs has been driven home to me by over a decade of teaching in church-related colleges, Protestant and Catholic. When mainline Protestant and Catholic Christians, in a matter-of-fact way, cite John 3:16 or WWJD (What Would Jesus Do?) as shorthand for the essential Christian message, and when non-Christian individuals routinely define *religion* as one's personal relationship with God, the incredible success of the evangelical tradition in America is dramatically apparent.

For the purposes of this book, a more precise and historically grounded definition of the reality is necessary. Evangelicalism first emerged as a particular style of Protestant Christianity in
the English-speaking world during the middle of the eighteenth
century.[15] Continental pietism and British Puritanism set the stage
for the movement. Anglican clergy John Wesley and George
Whitefield, along with colonial New England's foremost theologian Jonathan Edwards, gave it spiritual depth and intellectual
potential. By the middle of the nineteenth century, evangelicalism, or revivalism as it was sometimes dubbed, had left an indeli-
ble mark on formal and popular religion in the United States.
From the White House to the slave quarter, it permeated nearly
every aspect of American culture. Historian Randall Balmer
speaks of American evangelicalism as a national "folk religion."[16]

Today evangelicalism spans the globe as an international
Christian movement. It embraces millions of believers in a host of
evangelical denominations and independent churches as well as
many other adherents affiliated with churches whose creeds are
not officially evangelical in character. Estimates of the contemporary U.S. evangelical population range from 44 to 126 million.
According to the Institute for the Study of American Evangelicals
at Wheaton College, evangelicals in 2005 constituted about 35
percent of the total U.S. population—approximately 100 million
individuals. A Gallup poll conducted that same year reported that
42 percent of all Americans surveyed identified themselves as
"born again."[17]

For over two centuries, the distinguishing feature of the
evangelical tradition has been an intentional privileging of the
experiential dimension of religion. Evangelicals believe that a
profound personal conversion, often described as being "born
again" or making a "decision for Christ," outranks all other mea-
surements of authentic Christian identity—moral, doctrinal, ritual, and ecclesiastical. John Wesley's famous reference to his
"strangely warmed" heart captures the essence of this experience-
focused and salvation-centered way of being Christian. Three

other key factors in evangelicalism's makeup, according to a widely accepted scheme developed by British historian David Bebbington, include a strong emphasis on scripture as the ultimate authority for faith and practice, a penchant for the activist ministries of evangelism and missions, and a preoccupation with soteriology—a tendency to see the cross, more than any other symbol or theological category, as the core of Christianity's message of redemption.[18]

Beyond these basic distinctives, however, worldwide evangelicalism exhibits impressive diversity. It is by nature neither liberal nor conservative, neither intellectual nor emotional, neither politically engaged nor quietist. Like other Christians, evangelicals divide over issues such as abortion, homosexuality, women in ministry, church polity, sacraments, church and state, the environment, war and peace, economic globalization, and the interpretation of scripture. A growing presence in South America, sub-Sahara Africa, and southern and eastern Asia, global evangelicalism is united by no particular cultural agenda or set of social values.

American evangelicalism displays the same sort of variety. Public figures who are evangelicals—such as George W. Bush, Bill Clinton, Al Gore, John Ashcroft, Chuck Colson, Jesse Jackson, Al Sharpton, and Jimmy Carter—represent a wide spectrum of interests and concerns. Pop culture notables boasting "born again" credentials—such as action star Chuck Norris, former porn-star Linda Lovelace, television celebrity Mr. T, shock-rocker Alice Cooper, and motorcycle daredevil Evel Knievel—also provide convincing evidence of American evangelicalism's internal plurality. Elder statesmen in the movement—Billy Graham, Oral Roberts, Pat Robertson, James Dobson, Tim LaHaye, Charles Stanley, James Kennedy, and the like—continue to gravitate toward right-wing and, at times, theocratic values. The big tent of contemporary American evangelical leadership, however, accommodates not only the prime-time evangelicalism of T. D. Jakes and Joel Osteen but also the classical confessionalism of John Piper and Al Mohler, the "seeker-sensitive" pragmatism of

Bill Hybels and Rick Warren, the countercultural activism of Jim Wallis and Ronald Sider, and the "emerging" experimentalism of Brian McLaren and Leonard Sweet. An enormous breadth of belief and perspective defines the current shape of America's evangelical community.[19]

Modernity and Modernism

Working definitions are also needed for a set of related terms: *modern, modernity,* and *modernism.* As a concept and as a reality, fundamentalism is dependent upon all three. Quantitatively speaking, *modern* refers to the period of Western history inaugurated in the seventeenth or eighteenth century. Associated with the Enlightenment, or the Age of Reason, it describes the post-medieval world engendered by a series of paradigm shifts that dramatically transformed Western Christian society. These shifts include the scientific, philosophical, political, commercial, industrial, technological, military, aesthetic, and eventually sexual revolutions that created the post-Christian secular city now so familiar to virtually every human affected by mass electronic culture. Some scholars fix the end of the modern period in the twentieth century. Some speak of a postmodern period arising after World War II. For simplicity's sake, I see modern history as unfolding in phases or chapters, with our current experience as simply another stage of the dynamic and ever-changing modern project.

Qualitatively, *modern* overlaps with the more complex concept *modernity.* The latter term expresses the inward or subjective dimension of modern experience. It draws attention to the psychological conditions necessary for modern history and the process of modernization. Not a set of identifiable ideas, still less a creed, it refers more properly to a frame of mind, a way of thinking, a set of assumptions that can be called modern consciousness. Historians and social scientists differ with each other as to exactly what constitutes the modern state of mind. Many locate it in the cognitive tension between a sense of unlimited personal freedom and the reality of a society dominated by massive bureaucratic organizations. All agree that modernity represents the mental condition in which history, tradition, fate, and authority have been profoundly relativized or negated. Though tied to the unique history of the Western imagination, for almost two centuries modernity has proved to be eminently portable—even contagious. Sorting out the correlation between modernization and the phenomena of Westernization and globalization is part of an ongoing scholarly debate.

Images of instability and exhilaration permeate the critical discourse on modernity. Borrowing from Karl Marx, political theorist Marshall Berman speaks of modernity as "a maelstrom of perpetual disintegration and renewal," conflicted participation in a universe in which "all that is solid melts into air."[20] Sociologist Peter Berger has defined modernity as the "heretical imperative"—the liberating yet sometimes paralyzing sense of the infinite pluralization of choices.[21] Whether this state of mind is seen as positive or negative, of course, depends ultimately upon one's vantage point. Fundamentalists, as we will see, are moderns who find modernity particularly disturbing.

Not every antimodernist qualifies as a fundamentalist, though. An undercurrent of antimodernist discontent flows beneath much of modern thought. Antiurbanism and anti-industrialism, features of a longstanding arcadian myth in Western consciousness, have found articulate advocates in figures ranging from William Wordsworth, Thomas Jefferson, and Henry David Thoreau to historian Lynn White, writer J. R. R. Tolkien, and poet Wendell Berry.[22] Doctors of modern suspicion Friedrich Nietzsche and Sigmund Freud likewise registered deep reservations about "our whole unhealthy modernity."[23] George Orwell, author of the antitotalitarianism novels *Animal Farm* (1945) and *Nineteen Eighty-Four* (1949), spoke for many when he lamented "the ugliness and spiritual emptiness of the machine age."[24] T. S. Eliot, whose poem *The Waste Land* (1922) captured the lost generation's disillusionment with things modern, called "modern material civilisation" a "living death."[25] Members of the relatively understudied Traditionalist school of philosophy — such as Rene Guenon, Frithjof Schuon, Ananda Coomaraswamy, and Julius Evola — sought to recover a *sophia perennis* buried under the rubble of modernity's misguided idolatries. Huston Smith and Seyyed Hossein Nasr, preeminent representatives of that school today, continue to prophesy with gentle wisdom against the "spiritual poverty" of the modern milieu.[26] Other critiques have focused on the allegedly rootless, frenetic, fragmented, and one-dimensional qualities of modern life. Many have complained of the inordinate commodification of life in modern society. Few historians have reckoned seriously with this antimodern dimension of the modern experience. Future initiatives in fundamentalism studies should investigate the possible connections between secular and religious critiques of modernity.

The third term in our triad, *modernism,* describes an ideological response to things modern and modernity itself. In art, architecture, literature, and music, the word evokes a range of varied meanings and an array of period styles rejecting the normativity of classical models. In theology it refers principally to movements within late nineteenth- and early twentieth-century Protestant and Catholic intellectual culture that sought to reconcile Christian tradition with the basic assumptions of modern thought. The chief centers for Protestant modernism were Germany and the United States. Catholic modernists worked mainly in France and England, with a handful in America. Despite their religious and cultural differences, both Protestant and Catholic modernists aimed at two basic goals: (1) opening the study of Christianity to historical consciousness and scientific procedures, and (2) liberating that study from institutional church control. If we take them at their word, we should also mention a third objective: saving Christianity from extinction. Though seen as dissidents in their respective religious communities, both Protestant and Catholic modernists maintained that their unconventional efforts issued from the purest of apologetic motives. For them, rising levels of literacy and education, plus general acceptance of the scientific worldview, made it necessary to adapt Christianity to modern times. If Christianity did not change, they argued, it would die.

By extension, *modernism* can signify any attempt in any religion to translate faith and practice into modern terms. Often it carries with it the additional meaning of trying to evaluate traditional faith by modern standards. The Reform movement in Judaism, feminist ventures in Islam, and neo-Hindu universalisms calibrated for Western tastes offer examples of the multiple incarnations of the modernist spirit in world religions.

As we will see, the fundamentalisms covered in this book, from the Protestant archetype to the latest Islamic variation, have consistently defined themselves over against real or perceived modernist threats. Ironically, fundamentalism and modernism, though seemingly polar opposites, have much in common. Both are products of the modern period, and both are rooted (to different extents) in the Enlightenment legacy. Neither movement can be imagined outside the context of modernity. Both are also motivated by the desire to rescue a religious heritage in jeopardy. For fundamentalism, this means defense of true religion endangered by apostasy, unbelief, and secularism; for modernism, it means rescuing religion from irrelevance. Likewise, both movements are preoccupied with the task of identifying essentials. A cultural atmosphere in which "all that is solid melts into air" has no capacity for a *summa theologica*. Truth in the modern world of billboards, jingles, sound bites, and pop-up ads has to be lean. Finally, both modernism and fundamentalism exist in something of a symbiotic relationship with each other. While modernism, obsessed with the inadequacy of premodern orthodoxy, may arguably stand on its own, fundamentalism depends both historically and logically upon modernism. Without modernism, there would be no fundamentalism.

1
The Evangelical Roots
of Fundamentalism and
Fundamentalism Studies

According to conventional wisdom, fundamentalism has no history. As long as traditional Christianity has been around, we are told, fundamentalism, at least in latent form, has always existed. As long as some Christians have resisted cultural progress, minimized intellectual creativity, offered simplistic answers to complex questions, or expressed their faith in bigoted, intolerant, or even violent ways, fundamentalism has been a persistent factor in historical Christianity. What is labeled *fundamentalism* in society today, according to this way of thinking, represents a primitive type of precritical Christian faith surviving in a cultural environment hostile to the mindset of premodern religious belief. Consequently, the origins of fundamentalism, in so far as they are distinct from the genesis of traditional Christian doctrine, cannot be identified. Fundamentalism has no history and thus no real beginning.

These are common assumptions governing popular views of fundamentalism. They are especially evident in the familiar language that equates fundamentalism with "old-time religion" or that associates contemporary conservative Christianity with a return to fundamentalism. For several decades, the academic study of fundamentalism has systematically challenged these assumptions. If there is one thing that experts now agree on, it is this: fundamentalism does not constitute an eternal type of religious orientation found potentially in all historical periods and cultural contexts. Rather, it is a specific and culturally conditioned response to the intellectual and social challenges of modernity. The most striking discovery of fundamentalism studies has been the novelty of the fundamentalist phenomenon. Fundamentalism is not old; it is new.

This chapter and the next introduce the reader to the groundbreaking works that created the modern academic study of fundamentalism. They focus on seminal studies that have attempted to identify the sources of what is now known as the model for all other fundamentalisms: early twentieth-century North American Protestant fundamentalism. The scholars whose works are featured in these chapters concentrated on two basic issues: the historical origins of the fundamentalist movement and the precise nature of fundamentalism itself.

Before examining their work, however, we need to understand the cultural matrix that gave rise to both early fundamentalism and the first forays into the study of fundamentalism. First, we must have a firm grasp of the nature and dynamics of the evangelical tradition in U.S. culture, especially during the nineteenth century. Two important historical developments during that period made Protestant fundamentalism a cultural possibility: (1) evangelicalism's ascent to prominence in mainstream American culture and (2) the emergence of a growing wedge between conservative and liberal currents in evangelical intellectual life. Next, we must reckon with the challenges exerted by a new modernist movement in the nation's Protestant denominations and educational institutions. The reason for this is twofold. Fundamentalism originally materialized as a strategic response to modernism. At the same time, the first scholars to take fundamentalism seriously were self-proclaimed modernists.

Evangelicalism in American Culture

By the time fundamentalism first appeared on the American scene, evangelicalism had already enjoyed phenomenal success in the country's free market of religious ideas. The Great Awakening of the 1730s and 1740s established evangelicalism as a serious option for American Christians. George Whitefield fanned the flames of revival during seven evangelistic tours of the colonies, and Jonathan Edwards secured the "surprising work of God" a permanent and nearly mythic place in evangelical memory. After a second explosion of evangelical excitement, beginning with the frontier sacramental and camp meetings of the early nineteenth century, evangelicalism gradually became the prevailing American way of being Christian. Encompassing common and elite, Calvinist and Wesleyan, free and slave, it represented America's most culturally diverse and theologically pluralist religious movement. With its exaltation of the individual and its mistrust of institutions and the past, low-church evangelicalism seemed tailor-made for the young future-oriented democracy.[1]

Like any religious movement, however, the American evangelical tradition has always been a living organism, evolving over time, periodically renegotiating its relationship with culture, and experiencing increasing degrees of internal diversity.[2] After 1800, much of that change, adaptation, and diversity expressed itself in terms of the growing sectional consciousness pulling the country apart. In the North, America's original Bible Belt, evangelicalism accommodated itself to a climate of social reform and religious experimentation. Donald Dayton's classic *Discovering an Evangelical Heritage* (1976) captured a regional evangelicalism reinventing itself as it invested social resources into new antislavery and feminist crusades and intellectual capital into new ideas such as perfectionism.[3] For many historians, northern revivalist, reformer, and educator Charles Grandison Finney best exemplifies this genre of entrepreneurial evangelicalism, extending its influence into every realm of culture from politics and race to entertainment and diet.[4]

In the South, agrarian economics, greater religious homogeneity, and the "peculiar institution" of slavery took evangelicalism in different directions. Antebellum "gentlemen theologians" at the South's few educational institutions thought that their rational orthodoxy naturally entailed social stability and the spirituality of the church, not humanitarian agitation. In the back bayous and brush harbors of the "invisible institution," enslaved Africans and their descendants forged new evangelical Christianities out of cherished African traditions, biblical myth and prophecy, individual visionary experiences, and shared hope fixated on liberation in this world and the next. After slaveholding sliced the big three evangelical denominations (Methodist, Baptist, and Presbyterian) into regional bodies, each section thought that the controversy had vindicated its particular brand of evangelical faith for the "almost chosen" nation. In a sense, the American Civil War can be seen as one zealous evangelical nation fighting another.[5]

After the war, regional differences remained important. Defeat and Reconstruction helped push America's Bible Belt below the Mason-Dixon line. Southern whites redefined their evangelical heritage in terms of a new "Lost Cause" civil religion.[6] Black southerners, chastened by inequalities that outlived emancipation, developed distinctively evangelical survival strategies shaped by political disenfranchisement and Jim Crow legislation. Upstart Holiness and Pentecostal sects proliferated on both sides of the color line. Gradually, as the South became the "Solid South," it won its reputation as the most religious section of the country—to many Americans, a strange land of twilight tent meetings and jackleg preachers. As historian Sam Hill has pointed out, the South became the only place in world Christianity where evangelical Protestantism ruled as the dominant form of religion.[7] In the twentieth century, Catholic novelist Flannery O'Connor would describe her fellow southerners as "Christ-haunted."[8]

Meanwhile, immigration and urbanization chipped away at evangelical hegemony in the post–Civil War North. Catholic newcomers from southern and eastern Europe swelled the ranks of their Irish-dominated Church. Along with a rising tide of Ashkenazic Jews, they established highly visible ethnic enclaves in the nation's burgeoning industrial cities. The cities also brought forth new religious alternatives such as Mary Baker Eddy's Christian Science and Madame Blavatsky's Theosophy. At the same time, high-profile institutions, once monuments to evangelical identity and mission, fell victim to a process of secularization that eventually became rampant. The pattern is especially clear in the history of church-related higher education. Today at Finney's Oberlin College in Ohio, to cite just one example, evangelicalism exists more as an institutional relic than a guiding spirit.

The Divided Mind of American Evangelicalism

As important as these regional differences were, they paled in comparison with the growing ideological differences that split the American evangelical community during the second half of the nineteenth century. New fault lines in the tradition appeared, revealing divisions more profound than geography or politics. Advances in communication, transportation, and economic organization would eventually erode much of the sectional barrier in American evangelical life. The ideological chasm that opened up during this time, however, has remained a defining factor in American religious life ever since.

The key to understanding this division within the evangelical mind is the Enlightenment—or more properly, divergent attitudes toward the Enlightenment. Often called the Age of Reason, because of the premium its advocates placed on the role of critical, autonomous rationality, the Enlightenment revolutionized many aspects of Western civilization during the seventeenth and eighteenth centuries. Its cultural signature included a cluster of ideas and values that became part and parcel of the modern experience: scientific rationalism, philosophical naturalism, social-contract government, individual rights, laissez-faire economics, historical progress, and religious tolerance. In addition to reason, other catchwords of the movement were *liberty, nature, progress,* and *critique*—all humanist and this-worldly interests, all in stark contrast to the dominant themes (real or imagined) of medieval Christendom. Occurring primarily in Protestant nations, the Enlightenment fused with trends, already regnant within the Protestant ethos, emphasizing the integrity, rights, responsibilities, interior authority, and secular vocation of the individual person. This extraordinary synthesis of convictions, assumptions, instincts, and practices effectively produced what we call the modern worldview.[9]

From 1800 to the early decades of the twentieth century, American evangelicals struggled to define the precise nature of their status as modern Christians in the shadow of the Enlightenment. To what extent did modernity alter the meaning and content of Christian faith? In what ways did Christian commitment forestall full embrace of modern consciousness? Moreover, what exactly constituted "modern"? Was the Enlightenment simply a discrete, unrepeatable event—a historical boundary separating medieval superstition from modern rationality? Or did it represent more? Did the Enlightenment signal the inauguration of a new epoch of reform and revolution, still ongoing? Was it indeed the charter for endless critique? These are the questions that preoccupied the best minds in the evangelical movement during a critical phase of its American career.

During the eighteenth century, these questions resided below the level of consciousness. No evangelical rejected the Enlightenment out of hand. As a modern phenomenon itself, evangelicalism could hardly tolerate pure antimodernism. Despite the persistence of premodern folk beliefs and practices, all evangelicals since the Great Awakening inhabited an intellectual world structured by Enlightenment norms in one way or another. Natural selection and the age of the earth would spark heated intraevangelical debates after the 1850s, but no literate evangelical of the period questioned the validity of Copernicus's heliocentric theory or Newton's notion of gravitation. Evangelicals learned as a matter of course how to make the mental leap from the biblical world to their own, without ever casting doubt on the legitimacy of the paradigm shift that made a democratized modern scientific worldview a standard element in their life.

The career of Jonathan Edwards, America's premier evangelical intellectual, demonstrates how Enlightenment thought and evangelical spirituality represented two compatible options in early modern culture. As a strict Calvinist, Edwards was absolutely committed to Christian creed and biblical revelation. At the same time, he was thoroughly immersed in the intellectual life of his day, mastering modern natural philosophy on topics ranging from spiders and optics to what "sleeping rocks dream of." Nearly a century of critical scholarship has placed Edwards's command of the "new learning" beyond dispute. Though Perry Miller's famous reference to Edwards as "the most modern man of his age" has been hotly debated for decades, it has long been a truism in Edwards studies that his brilliant synthesis of Reformed divinity with the worldview of Newton and Locke stands peerless in the history of American letters. Edwards wove classical Christianity and modern thought into a seamless and stunningly original vision of reality. For him, as Miller put it, "there could be no warfare between religion and science."[10]

Edwards read the Enlightenment in the context of his doctrine of divine providence. Like the Reformation, the Enlightenment was a catalytic moment in God's sovereign rule of human history. Edwards even saw the universal spread of new thought as a sign of the dawning millennium. After his death in 1758, his spiritual children, though seemingly predestined to continue the harmonization of "new thought" and "new birth," could not effectively replicate his deft intellectual balancing act. Almost immediately they began to look upon the Enlightenment strain in their heritage in two different ways. Ultimately, they followed two diverse courses when it came to formulating a position on the uses of the Enlightenment. After Edwards, what divided evangelicals ideologically was not the Enlightenment itself but questions regarding the precise nature of its meaning and continuing relevance.

Conservative Evangelicalism

Part of the evangelical community took a path, dubbed "conservative" by default, which aligned the evangelical tradition with a strictly early modern approach to science and intellectual life. It perceived the Enlightenment to be a beneficial, perhaps even divinely ordained, flowering of human knowledge. It adopted the language of natural "laws," accepted the widespread application of empirical methods to virtually every dimension of life, and essentially baptized the scientific worldview. It even admitted that the collection and organization of data from the natural world might be a ceaseless activity, given the immensity of God's creation and the limitations of the human mind. It did not, however, see the Age of Reason as a mandate for open-ended critique of first principles, especially the fundamental tenets of Christian religion. Nor did it imagine that other "enlightenments" might possibly call into question certainties established by Newton and his contemporaries. In this sense, science, broadly conceived, constituted a relatively stable set of conclusions about God's created order—incomplete, yes, and always needing refinement, but authoritative and reliable nonetheless. Just as many Americans embraced the Enlightenment warrants for "1776" but drew the line when it came to future American revolutions, evangelicals taking this approach thought in terms of a single scientific revolution inaugurating a new age of rational (and still biblical) Christianity. What they did not—or could not— foresee was a situation of perpetual intellectual revolution.

In his magisterial study *The Enlightenment in America* (1976), historian Henry F. May called this position the didactic Enlightenment.[11] The didactic Enlightenment was an appropriation of modern thought intellectually less adventurous and politically more cautious than the moderate Enlightenment of Locke, the skeptical Enlightenment of Voltaire and Hume, and the revolutionary Enlightenment of Rousseau, Jefferson, and Paine. During the nineteenth century, cultural shape for the didactic Enlightenment was provided by the philosophical tradition known as common sense realism. Sometimes referred to as Scottish realism due to the nationality of its main architects, Aberdeen philosopher Thomas Reid and his student, Edinburgh philosopher Dugald Stewart, common sense realism became the philosophy of choice for generations of American Protestants. It was enshrined in America's major colleges and divinity schools and propagated by means of a long line of textbooks, sermons, tracts, and commentaries.[12]

Two features of the common sense philosophy made it especially appealing to conservative evangelicals. With its confidence in the capabilities of ordinary humans to discern sacred order in the natural world and the moral universe, it simultaneously blessed science, endorsed American democracy, shored up individual moral responsibility, and safeguarded traditional social values. Its apparent genius for defending traditional Christian claims with the same empirical methods made good by science enhanced the prestige of theology, legitimized belief in the supernatural, and buttressed popular assumptions regarding the evidences for Christianity. Church historian Sydney Ahlstrom once called it "an apologetic philosophy, *par excellence.*"[13] Common sense realism blended so effortlessly with the American Protestant ethos that it became a highly influential though nearly invisible presence in U.S. intellectual culture. Major histories by Mark Noll and Brooks Holifield have underscored the crucial place of the Scottish philosophy in the nation's developing theological tradition.[14]

One consequence of this partnership between evangelical spirituality and common sense thought was a reinforcement of evangelicalism's tendency toward individualism. According to the Scottish philosophy, the individual human being was the basic unit in temporal and eternal affairs. In matters both spiritual and civil, the individual person as sinner and citizen remained the focal point for evangelical life and thought. Especially after the Second Great Awakening, as Jacksonian populism fed evangelical assumptions, evangelical soteriology increasingly portrayed salvation in individualist terms. Even activism in antebellum evangelicalism's "benevolent empire" of charitable and reform causes was seen primarily as the consecrated work of regenerated individuals. Timothy L. Smith's *Revivalism and Social Reform* (1957) documented pre–Civil War evangelicalism's attempt to balance a social ethic and a salvationist gospel.[15] By the close of the nineteenth century, pastor-theologians such as Washington Gladden and Walter Rauschenbusch were beginning to develop new collective understandings of classical theological themes for the industrial age — arguing for the corporate and structural nature of sin and salvation, for example. Congregational minister and editor Charles M. Sheldon popularized this social gospel with his bestselling novel *In His Steps: What Would Jesus Do?* (1896).[16] Remnants of the once influential common sense philosophy, however, eventually fueled evangelical resistance to the social gospel — tainted as it was at times with departures from evangelical orthodoxy. The preeminent urban evangelist of the Victorian period, salesman-turned-revivalist Dwight L. Moody, perfected the techniques of "salvation as civic spectacle." Ironically he understood his mass gospel mission chiefly as "soul-winning" — rescuing lost sinners one by one.[17] For many conservative evangelicals, Prohibition became the only social cause worthy of Christian commitment.

Another important application of common sense realism came in the area of evangelical approaches to revelation and scripture. In light of the concept of the unity of truth undergirding the philosophical system, conservative evangelicals believed that scientific truth and self-evident truths of unaided reason corresponded flawlessly with truths already established by divine revelation. Genuine science and genuine rationality, by definition, could never contradict revelation, including the written record of revelation preserved in the Bible. Evangelicals remembered Pilgrim father John Robinson's dictum that "yet more light" may break forth from God's holy word, but they understood the remark in the context of the never-ending struggle to overcome the limits of human understanding, not the possibility of changes or contradictions in scripture. Not surprisingly, the specialized language of early modern science—*fact, evidence, certainty, credibility,* and *authenticity*—played a conspicuous role in the theological works produced by evangelicals of the period. Revelation was understood in terms of reasonable propositions, and the Bible was compared to a warehouse of facts. This was true across the entire spectrum of conservative evangelicalism—from Finney's *Lectures on Systematic Theology* (1846) to the *Systematic Theology* (1872–73) of his Princeton Seminary critic, Charles Hodge, spokesman for a more sober confessional, evangelical Calvinism. Theologians on both flanks of the conservative movement spoke of their discipline as an inductive science paralleling the natural sciences of chemistry and biology. Hodge's innovative doctrine of biblical inerrancy, destined to be the rallying cry of full-blown fundamentalism half a century later, was directly rooted in common sense realism.[18]

Evangelicals in this conservative wing of the movement also saw no conflict between their Enlightenment allegiances and an other-worldly theology of history characterized by a robust eschatology, or, study of "last things." It is well known that Isaac Newton balanced his conception of a cosmos governed by natural laws with an apocalyptic imagination fired by intense interest in the Book of Revelation. Colonial New England divines, too, combined early modern scientific thinking with intricate interpretations of biblical prophecy. Chiliasm or millennialism, based on belief in Christ's future thousand-year reign on earth (Rev 20), was a stock component of the Puritan intellectual legacy inherited by evangelicals. Most Puritan theologians endorsed the approach called premillennialism—the conviction that Christ's second coming would precede the millennial kingdom. Jonathan Edwards departed from that tradition, developing America's first comprehensive version of postmillennialism—placing the second advent after the expansion of Christ's terrestrial kingdom. During the nineteenth century, evangelicals debated the relative merits of both systems, with premillennialism eventually winning out as the trademark of conservative evangelical eschatology. When Irish nonconformist John Nelson Darby spread his new message of dispensational premillennialism in America during the 1860s and 1870s, he found an audience primed for doctrines of Christ's any-moment return and a rapture of the church. Little did he know he was sowing the seeds for the phenomenon of fundamentalism. Across the board, it was assumed that apocalyptic thought was fully consistent with the axioms of the didactic Enlightenment.

The Rise of Evangelical Liberalism

From East Coast college president to freelance frontier revivalist, every evangelical American of the nineteenth century was influenced in some way by common sense realism's didactic assimilation of Enlightenment thought. All were not satisfied with it, though. Some said they eventually outgrew it. These figures, the founders of Protestant liberalism and its spin-off, modernism, represent the other side of the intellectual chasm forming in the evangelical imagination. Conservative evangelicals looked to the Enlightenment as a fixed point, a potentially closed system of natural knowledge that shed new light on an ultimately closed system of revealed knowledge. Liberal evangelicals seized on the Enlightenment as the symbol of an unfinished process, an ever-expanding sphere of knowledge and faith.

Several developments in early modern Anglo-American religion, interacting with Enlightenment forces, set the stage for the liberal movement in American Protestantism. The latitudinarian or "broad church" trend in the Anglican tradition promoted intellectual freedom within an inclusive framework of liturgical and organizational unity. John Locke's argument for a "reasonable" Christianity made the case for a tolerant, doctrinally simple Christian faith, subject to rational scrutiny and free from metaphysical complexity. The left wing of the Puritan movement, drawing on earlier Radical Reformation themes, served as the fertile breeding ground for new ideas such as unitarianism, universalism, and Arminianism (belief in free will)—all crucial departures from the rigid Scholasticism of post-Reformation Calvinism.

In America liberal religion assumed a number of different forms. Early moderates such as Boston Congregationalist leaders Benjamin Colman and Charles Chauncy combined old-style Puritan sobriety with advocacy for intellectual autonomy—"free and catholick," as they said. Thomas Jefferson staked out a quiet and private radicalism, defiant of ecclesiastical authority and critical of dogmatic schemes that insulted human dignity and encouraged credulity. Unitarian founder William Ellery Channing directed the liberal stream into a structured channel. His 1819 sermon "Unitarian Christianity" articulated the cluster of themes that would become major signposts of the liberal tradition for years to come: the benevolent character of God, the moral integrity of human nature, respect for "honest and devout inquiry," and an emphasis on humanist methods in theological study. "Our leading principle," he said, "is this, that the Bible is a book written for men, in the language of men, and that its meaning is to be sought in the same manner as that of other books."[19]

Despite Channing's earnest efforts and to the dismay of liberals ever since, organized religious liberalism never really flourished in the United States. Jefferson's 1823 prediction that "there is not a young man now living in the U.S. who will not die a Unitarian"[20] has been confounded any number of times during nearly two centuries of subsequent American religious history. Today the descendant of Channing's denomination, the Unitarian Universalist Association, remains one of the tiniest groups on the books. At the same time, though, as principled support for freedom of conscience and the unhindered quest for truth, Protestant liberalism triumphed in U.S. culture. Never strictly a set of ideas, it represented more a frame or habit of mind, even a mood. The first volume of Gary Dorrien's narrative history trilogy *The Making of American Liberal Theology* (2001–6) brilliantly shows how Protestant liberalism became a cross-denominational phenomenon in the nineteenth century.[21]

Ralph Waldo Emerson, finding even Channing's Unitarian Christianity too confining, explored the unknown territory of a post-Christian liberalism. By contrast, Congregationalist contemporary Horace Bushnell incorporated the liberal spirit into the heart of conventional trinitarian Christianity. His emphasis on Christian nurture, instead of cataclysmic conversion, and on the poetic nature of religious language, as opposed to its cognitive specificity, earned him the title of father of American evangelical liberalism. Bushnell perpetuated the Edwardsean dual stress upon experiential piety and Enlightenment learning but filtered both through a set of sentiments engendered by the Romantic movement. He did not question the drive to establish religion on a rational basis but supplemented that concern with new insights into the affective and aesthetic dimensions of religion—all of which resonated well with evangelicalism's "warm heart" religion. Like his European counterpart Friedrich Schleiermacher, founder of continental Protestant liberalism, Bushnell turned to feeling as the mainspring for religious consciousness.

After the Civil War, the mantle of liberal leadership passed to some of the most prominent celebrity preachers in the new urban America. Along with advocates of the new social gospel, Congregationalist Henry Ward Beecher at Plymouth Church in Brooklyn and Phillips Brooks at Boston's Trinity Episcopal

Church skillfully and sometimes flamboyantly popularized the liberal cause. Behind the scenes (until heresy charges thrust them center stage), seminary professors such as Crawford Howell Toy, Charles A. Briggs, Egbert C. Smith, and Henry Preserved Smith blazed new trails in academic evangelical theology. Elizabeth Cady Stanton and America's first generation of ordained women clergy pioneered in the area of feminist theology.

A survey of the literature reveals that the foremost motif running through nineteenth-century liberal thought was growth or development. Even before Darwin appropriated the theme to communicate his scientific hypothesis of natural selection, evolutionary thinking had captured the imagination of a class of modern Christian intellectuals. *An Essay on the Development of Christian Doctrine* (1845) by Victorian England's Catholic convert-cardinal John Henry Newman and the bustling enterprise of *Dogmengeschichte* in Germany's formidable academic establishment epitomized the new trend in historical and theological studies.[22] *Organic change* and *gradual progress* especially became the watchwords of the liberal trajectory in American Protestantism. Pilgrims along this path applied developmental theory to every aspect of civilization, including religion.

Convinced that each generation of believers must renew credibility for faith by calibrating the Christian message to the needs of its age, liberal evangelicals, like other Protestant liberals, hoped to sort out the enduring and transient themes in Christianity. Balancing continuity with the past with openness to an unfinished faith, they christened their approach "progressive orthodoxy" or simply the "new theology." Liberal evangelicals, whatever the moniker, perceived both the Enlightenment and Christian faith as works in progress. On principle committed to change, they expected, and sought, revision and redefinition in matters related to society and science, church and creed. Such sentiments paved the way for evangelical acceptance of Darwin's theory of biological evolution. As pastor-editor Lyman Abbott put it, evolution—presumably in all spheres of reality—was "God's way of doing things."[23] If familiar with Bernard Lonergan's notion of a "Second Enlightenment,"[24] liberal evangelicals would have heartily welcomed the idea of multiple or serial enlightenments.

The leading edge of this evolutionary approach to Christian faith was the practice of the higher criticism of the Bible. So-called lower criticism had been around since the Renaissance, as a growing collection of ancient manuscripts had forced scholars to develop comparative methods designed to evaluate texts on the basis of reliability and authenticity. An erudite craft unknown to rank-and-file believers, it never scandalized sensitive souls. Higher criticism, on the other hand, generated intense controversy by challenging cherished understandings of the inspiration and authority of the Bible.

The main point of this historical-critical method, according to its practitioners, was the application of modern inductive procedures to the study of the Bible. Higher critics borrowed the latest insights and techniques from history, philology, literary analysis, natural science, and the emerging fields of anthropology, archaeology, sociology, psychology, and comparative religion. They also accepted current standards of argumentation based on rational scrutiny, accurate documentation, and empirically verifiable evidence.

On the basis of rhetoric alone, however, it would be difficult to differentiate liberal biblical scholars from their conservative counterparts. Both claimed to be performing scientific study of the Bible, and both saw the enterprise as fully congruent with the modern spirit. What really set the higher critics apart was their starting point. Taking their cue from figures such as Leopold von Ranke, founder of the German scientific school of historiography, and Oxford's Sanskrit scholar Max Müller, who dreamed of a comparable science of religion, the higher critics aimed for a pristine level of objectivity, unsullied by the moralism, hagiography, and proof-texting that they thought characteristic of traditional biblical interpretation.

Rather than beginning with assumptions of the Bible's distinctive nature, the higher critics removed the Bible from its protected status as a special case and began to treat it like any other piece of literature. They envisioned the Bible as a collection of ancient texts, written in a variety of genres, produced by numerous authors and redactors, shaped by the conventions of oral cultures, and, perhaps most important, grounded in the ancient Near East's premodern cosmologies of myth and symbol. While conservative biblical theologians collected and systematized propositional truths enclosed within a divinely inspired text, higher critics raised critical questions about the text itself. They raised questions about Moses's authorship of the Pentateuch, the future orientation of Old Testament prophecy, the apostolic authorship of the Gospels and New Testament letters, and the historical authenticity of biblical miracles—at every step undercutting time-honored views regarding the Bible's integrity and uniqueness.

Unlike earlier rationalist approaches to the Bible, such as those associated with Paine, Jefferson, and a long line of freethinkers and village atheists, higher criticism was not born out of a spirit of skepticism or unbelief. It was almost exclusively the work of devout clergy-scholars opposed to undisciplined speculation and comfortable with a tentative faith. Holding key posts in prestigious seminaries and church-related universities, they influenced generations of young ministers and precipitated what one historian has called "the spiritual crisis of the Gilded Age."[25]

Jerry Wayne Brown's *The Rise of Biblical Criticism in America* (1969) remains a trustworthy history of the first generations of liberal Protestant biblical interpretation in the United States. It traces the development of the approach from the work of "Unitarian pope" Andrews Norton to the "foreign invasion" of radical European scholarship in the 1840s.[26] Scientific higher biblical criticism was perfected in the seminar rooms of modern German universities after 1850. It entered U.S. culture through the Ivy League divinity schools, denominational schools such as Methodism's Boston University and Presbyterianism's Union

Seminary, and eventually new institutions such as the University of Chicago, bankrolled by Baptist layman John D. Rockefeller. Where higher criticism took root, the phenomenon of theological modernism soon began to appear.

The Modernist Impulse

The origins of the term *modernism* are obscure—much less clear, ironically, than the origins of *fundamentalism*. Although the term has an extensive range of meanings in art, literature, and music, many historians believe that the term originated within the context of the theological ferment agitating European Catholic thought in the early twentieth century. In fact, it may have been Pope Pius X's 1907 condemnation of the amorphous movement he called "modernism" that gave the term its currency in the theological lexicon. In *Medievalism* (1909), excommunicated priest-theologian George Tyrrell supposed that the pope himself had invented the term.[27] Whatever its origins, the term eventually caught on in America, earning a confirmed place in public discourse by the 1920s.

The exact boundary between liberalism and modernism is hard to locate. Both movements shared a cluster of tenets attributable to the creative interface of Protestantism and the Enlightenment: intellectual self-reliance, the primacy of experience, critical approaches to the study of religion, an evolutionary view of history, and the complementarity of religion and science. But while liberals leaned toward pastoral concerns, moral cultivation, and vague doctrinal language, modernists tended to be more scientific in orientation and more categorical in their endorsement of historicism, the thesis that all religious experience is culturally conditioned. In his landmark study *The Modernist Impulse in American Protestantism* (1976), historian William R. Hutchison distinguished between the broad liberal desire to reconcile religion with modern culture and the more explicit modernist mission to adapt religion to modern ideas and standards.[28] For liberals, the Enlightenment represented intellectual and spiritual elbow room. For modernists, it became emblematic of a new theological criterion. As R. Scott Appleby has observed, the Protestant modernists "differed from other liberals by the level of self-awareness with which they appropriated the modern. They accomplished deliberately what others had attempted without self-conscious and sustained reference to modernity, namely, the recasting of the gospel in terms of what was then modern thought."[29]

Hutchison's work made it clear that evangelicals played a vital role in the formation of American modernism. Two Baptist scholars associated with the University of Chicago Divinity School grant us special insight into the early phase of the movement. If not the father of modernism, Maine native Shailer Mathews was at least one of its original patrons. The product of historical and sociological training in Berlin, he joined the Chicago faculty in 1894, just two years after the school opened its doors. Though originally hired to teach New Testament, Mathews eventually contributed to every area of theological research, especially historical theology. He edited the journal *Biblical World* and published over twenty books. A fervent apologist for the social gospel, he was also a committed churchman and ecumenist, serving as both president of the Northern Baptist Convention and first president of the Federal Council of Churches. As dean of the divinity school, Mathews recruited Canadian-born Shirley Jackson Case to join the Chicago faculty in 1908. Educated at Yale, Case taught New Testament interpretation and early church history for over two decades until assuming the dean's position following Mathews's retirement. More of a specialist than Mathews, Case concentrated on biblical studies and historical Jesus studies.

Together Mathews and Case made Chicago a thriving center for Protestant modernism—"a sort of modernist headquarters," as Hutchison noted.[30] Along with fellow modernist theologian Gerald Birney Smith, they inaugurated a new school of American religious thought called empirical theology, or simply the Chicago

School. Inspired by the pragmatism of William James and John Dewey and its "culture of inquiry," they endeavored to shift the focus of academic Christian theology toward an empirical examination of Christianity as a social, historical process. Their goal was not interpretation of doctrine, much less penetration into metaphysical truths expressed by doctrinal formulas, but rather understanding of how "group belief" actually functioned in the lives of people coming to terms with the specific challenges of their social and cosmic environments. Bringing the evangelical tradition full circle, Mathews and Case attempted to construct a "usable" theology on the basis of experience alone. Without reference to an authoritative church, an infallible canon, a "static body of truth," or an objective, transcendent, supernatural deity, they sought to translate James's concern for the instrumental "cash value" of beliefs into a coherent, postrealist theological strategy.[31]

According to a historian of this school, *empirical* meant three things for Mathews and Case: (1) a temperamental inclination toward concrete experience as opposed to abstract ideas, (2) a specific method of inquiry designed to collect and interpret data derived from experience, and (3) a willingness to acknowledge ordinary human experience as a source, guide, and authority for theological reflection.[32] Case applied this functional approach to his study of the sociohistorical environment fostering the early Christian movement and its literature. Mathews gravitated toward the practical consequences of religion in the lives of his fellow moderns. In *The Faith of Modernism* (1924), he defined modernism as *"the use of scientific, historical, social method in understanding and applying evangelical Christianity to the needs of living persons."*[33]

Toward Fundamentalism Studies

Mathews and Case were transitional figures in the history of American religious thought. Their works did not enjoy an impressive shelf life, nor did their brand of modernism fare very well after another "foreign invasion" (this time Karl Barth's neo-orthodoxy) transformed the American theological scene in the 1920s. James and Dewey exercised a more profound impact on American intellectual life, and the barnstorming evangelist and former Major League slugger Billy Sunday achieved greater celebrity than the college baseball star and modernist dean Shailer Mathews could ever imagine.

Nevertheless, the modernists' legacy has lived on in a number of different ways. They successfully ushered the liberal wing of the evangelical tradition into the prosperity of mainline Protestantism, and their influence is still felt in the worldwide ecumenical movement and the wider ecumenism of interreligious dialogue. They also performed the intellectual spadework for notable future initiatives such as process theology and the establishment of religious studies as an independent academic discipline.

Mathews and Case must be credited with at least one other, long-lasting, scholarly accomplishment. As students of culture, both men were keenly attentive to the signs of the times. Both knew that conservative American evangelicalism was on a collision course with post-Enlightenment modernity, and both realized that the two factions within evangelical Christianity were destined for a full-scale showdown. They recognized the significance of premillennialism's growing popularity and threw their scholarly energies into the attempt to comprehend the motives behind the antievolution crusade, then seriously building steam. As we will see in the following chapter, modernists Mathews and Case not only witnessed the birth of fundamentalism; to a certain extent, they invented fundamentalism studies.

2
The Birth and Rebirth
of Fundamentalism Studies

The study of North American Protestant fundamentalism did not begin as a formal area of academic specialization. It started as an exercise in occasional theology. Scholars interrupted demanding research and teaching agendas to respond to new ideas and events disrupting the status quo in church and culture. At first, it was purely an improvised art. No consensus on standards, criteria, or methodology existed, and the climate for study was often poisoned by polemics and acrimony. Like fundamentalism itself, the study of fundamentalism was born in a time of fierce internecine conflict. High-profile heresy trials and high-stakes denominational battles profoundly altered the environment for theological reflection and debate. In many cases, reputations, friendships, and careers were on the line.

Since the 1920s, the era that church historians have labeled the period of the fundamentalist-modernist controversy, the study of Protestant fundamentalism has changed enormously. The first scholars to engage in the study of fundamentalism laced descriptive analysis with theological critique. Most were modernist theologians who stepped into untested waters and launched what eventually became an international, interdisciplinary enterprise.

Their models for the interpretation of fundamentalism dominated scholarly opinion for nearly half a century.

The next generation of fundamentalism scholars, publishing during the 1960s, 1970s, and early 1980s, initiated a new, second, phase of the enterprise. Neither modernists nor theologians, they were professionally trained historians. Many had personal connections to evangelical or fundamentalist Christianity. The leading figures in this phase, in fact, tended to fit the profile of the former insider who combines empathy for his or her subject with mastery of the academy's methodological agnosticism. Functioning as a cultural bridge between conservative evangelicalism and mainstream academia, these scholars established fundamentalism studies as a respectable area of historical investigation. They also sparked a renaissance of historical interest in fundamentalist circles.

Since the 1980s, rising levels of disciplinary diversity, intellectual creativity, and methodological sophistication have characterized the third, and present, stage of the study of Protestant fundamentalism. New research strategies, especially those informed by feminist and comparative perspectives, have called into question previously accepted conclusions about the roots of the fundamentalist movement and have shed new light on the nature of the original fundamentalist impulse. In addition, new perspectives on the study of religion have made the religious affiliation of the researcher increasingly irrelevant.

This chapter traces the first two stages of the development of Protestant fundamentalism studies—from modernist theological appraisal to critical yet empathetic history. The following chapter covers the transition from the second, historical, stage to the third, and contemporary, pluralistic phase. Throughout nearly a century of existence, the study of classical Protestant fundamentalism has followed a course not unlike that of fundamentalism itself. Born in controversy and strife, fundamentalism studies has alternated between seasons of declension and renewal.

The Birth of Fundamentalism

For most of Christian history, a new religious movement has had to suffer the indignity of being named by its opponents. Lutherans, Anabaptists, Puritans, Quakers, Methodists, Shakers, Mormons, and a host of other groups, including perhaps even modernists, have been forced to accept labels concocted by their critics. Often these names, intended as instruments of abuse, have been transformed by their bearers into badges of honor.

Curiously, especially given its current derogatory meaning, fundamentalism was named by its adherents, not its first academic observers or theological foes. It took several decades, however, for the name to develop in the collective evangelical imagination. Since the late nineteenth century, conservative evangelical rhetoric had betrayed a growing preoccupation with the notion of non-negotiable, foundational beliefs. The interdenominational Niagara Bible Conferences, held in Ontario from the 1870s to 1900, introduced the language of "fundamentals" into evangelical discourse with a fourteen-point creed advocating biblical inerrancy and premillennial eschatology. Then, in 1910, the northern Presbyterian Church (U.S.A.) drafted doctrinal norms for its clergy, mandating belief in the so-called five points: the inspiration and inerrancy of the Bible, the virgin birth of Christ, the sacrificial quality of Christ's atoning death, the physical resurrection of Christ, and the supernatural character of New Testament miracles.

Next, a series of pamphlets financed by wealthy evangelical laymen Lyman and Milton Stewart reinforced the effort to define and defend theological basics. Published in twelve volumes between 1910 and 1915, these essays entitled *The Fundamentals: A Testimony to the Truth* expressed mounting evangelical concern over issues such as higher criticism, the erosion of traditional belief, Darwinism, and the proliferation of new religious options.[1] By 1919, the concept of fundamentals enjoyed such authority in the evangelical mind that Minnesota-based Baptist activist William Bell Riley declared his fledgling premillennialist and antievolution parachurch organization to be the World's Christian Fundamentals Association.[2]

Finally, on July 1, 1920, the word *fundamentalist* appeared in print for the first time. Its creator was Curtis Lee Laws, minister and editor of the Northern Baptist newspaper *The Watchman-Examiner.* Alarmed by the "rising tide of liberalism and rationalism" in the Northern Baptist Convention (NBC), Laws organized a caucus of conservative Baptist leaders prior to the denomination's 1920 summer convention in Buffalo. The purpose of the gathering, according to his paper, was "to restate, reaffirm, and reemphasize the fundamentals of our New Testament faith." Three thousand delegates attended the preconvention conference, and, as one historian put it, its effect on the NBC was "electric."[3] Afterward, Laws reflected on the larger meaning of the unprecedented events. Like Adam in Eden, he expanded the lexicon to make room for a new creature in the theological garden:

> We here and now move that a new word be adopted to describe the men among us who insist that the landmarks shall not be removed. "Conservatives" is too closely allied with reactionary forces in all walks of life. "Premillennialists" is too closely allied with a single doctrine and not sufficiently inclusive. "Landmarkers" has a historical disadvantage and connotes a particular group of radical conservatives. We suggest that those who still cling to the great fundamentals and who mean to do battle royal for the fundamentals shall be called "Fundamentalists."[4]

The companion word *fundamentalism* made its debut in 1921. "The name of the movement is a mere incident and is relatively unimportant," Laws wrote. "The movement itself will never die, because always there will be men brave enough to contend earnestly for the faith delivered once for all to the saints."[5] During the next few years, a number of "brave" leaders in the emerging movement—especially New York–based Baptist reformer John Roach Straton with his Fundamentalist League (1922) and Texas Baptist firebrand J. Frank Norris with his *Fundamentalist* newspaper (1927)—enthusiastically adopted the novel vocabulary, virtually canonizing the new terms as shibboleths of Christian orthodoxy.[6]

The Birth of Fundamentalism Studies

Ironically, the academic study of fundamentalism predated its official christening. Writing before Laws introduced his neologisms, Chicago modernists Mathews and Case identified premillennialism, not the quest for doctrinal fundamentals, as the real driving force behind the new militancy on the evangelical right flank. In the theological contests of the nineteenth century, premillennialism had steadily gained ground on postmillennialism. Evangelist D. L. Moody sanctioned it, and scores of Bible and prophecy conferences popularized it. By 1900, liberal and modernist theologians in mainline divinity schools began to take it quite seriously. From their vantage point, premillennialism represented an intricate and rather eccentric eschatological vision that entailed at least nine main beliefs: (1) the gradual deterioration of human civilization; (2) the invisibility of the true church; (3) the any-moment return of Christ; (4) the secret rapture of the church; (5) a period of tribulation marked by the rise of the Antichrist; (6) the return of the Jews to their ancient homeland and the conversion of some to Christianity; (7) the earthly rule of Christ and his saints for a thousand years; (8) a climactic battle with the forces of Satan; and (9) a final judgment heralding parallel eternities of heaven and hell.

Mathews, who had already published a monograph on messianic hope in the New Testament, addressed premillennialism briefly in a tract printed by the American Institute of Sacred Literature in 1917. He noted the parallels between premillennialist thought and ancient Jewish expectations but judged both virtually meaningless for modern Christians.[7] A year later, Case treated premillennialism more extensively in an article "The Premillennial Menace" and in a full-length study *The Millennial Hope* (1918).

Both Mathews and Case viewed premillennialism primarily as a set of ideas. Neither aggressively pursued questions of its historical origin or cultural background—issues that would later preoccupy scholars of fundamentalism.

The frank purpose of Case's book was to expose what he called premillennialism's "fallacious and harmful character." The burden of his argument focused on two major points: (1) the failure of premillennialists to discriminate properly among the various types of apocalyptic material in the Bible and (2) the ultimate irrelevance of any sort of biblical eschatology for modern Christian living. All previous millennial schemes had miscarried, Case observed, and all had been tainted by "fanciful content" unsuitable for the modern scientific mind. Case also accused premillennialism of fostering a pessimistic view of history and a fatalistic approach to social problems. Writing in the context of World War I, he found these elements of the system especially disturbing. Premillennialism's "negative attitude," he concluded, "becomes peculiarly vicious in the present hour of the world's need, when the call to duty is no longer merely local, but nation-wide and international."[8]

The modernist analysis of premillennialist biblical interpretation became a standard feature of the first academic assessments of fundamentalism. So did the modernist indictment of premillennialism's social philosophy. After the rapid acceptance of *fundamentalism* as the primary label for the new phenomenon of conservative evangelical activism, these two interpretive strategies fanned out into a multifaceted research effort aimed at the study of partisan conservative Christianity. With that, fundamentalism studies was born.

Modernist Models

During the 1920s and 1930s, modernist and liberal theologians experimented with three explanatory hypotheses designed to capture the dynamics of fundamentalism in a conceptual framework. All three demonstrated a significant degree of intellectual dependence upon the new social sciences. The first hypothesis, a clash of cultures model, portrayed modernism and fundamentalism as mirror images of each other—competing Christianities staking out diametrically opposed positions on religion and modernity. A second approach, the rural-urban theory (with a southern-northern variant, popular after the 1925 *Scopes* trial) depicted fundamentalism as a religious orientation profoundly alienated from the ambience of modern city life, an agrarian rebellion against industrial modernity. A third option, the cultural lag thesis, pictured fundamentalists as Christians who had been left behind by the Western world's rapid advance toward modernization. Fundamentalism, it suggested, was an outdated faith from an earlier phase of social development living on borrowed time.

The two-cultures or two-Christianities theory achieved definitive articulation in the work of Shailer Mathews and his Chicago colleague, church historian William Warren Sweet, who endorsed it in his influential textbook *The Story of Religion in America* (1939).[9] In *The Faith of Modernism* (1924), Mathews reduced the fundamentalist-modernist controversy to a "struggle between two types of mind, two attitudes toward culture, and, in consequence, two conceptions as to how Christianity can help us live." The difference between these "two types of Christians," he said, turned on contrary definitions of religion and notions of authority. Fundamentalists were "Confessional or Dogmatic" Christians committed to a strictly theological definition of religion. They equated religion with adherence to specific sets of ideas revealed by God and ratified by authoritative figures in the past. Modernists, by contrast, minimized the cognitive content of religion, emphasizing its moral and subjective dimensions instead. They located authority in the experience of the present. Ever the historian, Mathews viewed fundamentalism and modernism as twin products of a new phase of differentiation in Christian history. In another age, he speculated, they might well have been separate religious orders or special-purpose denominations. Ever the statesman, Mathews saw the movements as complementary Christian apostolates. "If, like Peter they have the duty of evangelizing one type of persons," he wrote, "we like Paul have the duty of evangelizing another."[10]

The rural-urban and cultural lag models found numerous adherents during the 1920s—from Dartmouth sociologist John Mecklin to French political scientist Andre Siegfried.[11] The models gained classic expression in the works of an American theologian outside the Chicago circle: Missouri-born, Yale-educated H. Richard Niebuhr. Though sometimes uncritically associated with neo-orthodoxy's assault upon Protestant liberalism, Niebuhr shared many of the same values that animated the Chicago modernists. Today his critique of the liberal "Christ without a cross" is widely recognized as a caricature of nineteenth-century theology.[12] His first major work, *The Social Sources of Denominationalism* (1929), interpreted the fundamentalist-modernist controversy in terms of a perennial "conflict between urban and rural religion." Drawing upon the still largely unknown theories of German sociologist Max Weber, Niebuhr contrasted "rural Fundamentalism" with "bourgeois Modernism," linking the former to "the memories and habits of frontier faith."[13] When he contributed an entry on fundamentalism to the first *Encyclopedia of the Social Sciences* (1930–35), edited by economists Edwin Seligman and Alvin Johnson, the rural-urban interpretation had risen to near-orthodox status in the scholarly community. Academic historians, such as Charles and Mary Beard, had already begun to exploit it routinely. Eventually, as James Thompson has noted, it became "entrenched in the scholarly and popular mind."[14] According to Niebuhr, fundamentalism was most prevalent in "those isolated communities in which the traditions of pioneer society had been most effectively preserved and which were least subject to the influence of modern science and industrial civilization."[15]

In his mature theological works, however, Niebuhr gradually distanced himself from the rural-urban scheme. He relied increasingly on the cultural lag thesis, using *fundamentalism* more as a byword than a technical, descriptive category. In *The Meaning of Revelation* (1941), for example, he called fundamentalism a theological "lost cause." In his masterpiece *Christ and Culture* (1951), he dismissed it as loyalty to "old cultural ideas."[16] Other makers of the mid-twentieth-century American theological mind followed suit. Paul Tillich found American fundamentalism to be a fossilized orthodoxy committed to "the theological truth of yesterday." Niebuhr's famous theologian brother Reinhold saw nothing in it but an outworn creed "bound to end in futility."[17]

All three of the modernists' explanatory hypotheses informed the arguments of the first comprehensive scholarly treatment of fundamentalism: Stewart Grant Cole's *History of Fundamentalism* (1931). A protégé of Chicago's Gerald Birney Smith, Cole wrote his 1929 dissertation on "The Psychology of the Fundamentalist Movement." After graduation, he put his teacher's empirical theology to work in a number of venues during a long and varied career. He contributed to the science-religion dialogue, published in the area of intercultural education, and labored tirelessly in the cause of interfaith and race relations. His history of fundamentalism, styled as a "clinical investigation" of Christianity in the crucible of secularization, represented the first serious attempt to place the entire phenomenon of fundamentalism into a coherent historical and theological context. It remained the benchmark in the field well into the 1950s.[18]

Cole organized his history around the two-cultures theme. Like his other mentor, Mathews, he saw fundamentalism and modernism as rival Christianities contending for what each fervently thought to be the essence of authentic faith. The conflict between the two movements, he stated, amounted to a "clash of Christian cultures." In support of that thesis, Cole gathered an impressive amount of data never before assembled to address three main issues: (1) the rise of fundamentalism; (2) fundamentalist agitation in five denominations (Northern Baptist, Presbyterian, Disciples, Methodist, and Episcopal); and (3) fundamentalist campaigns in secular society. Fundamentalism, he concluded, was

a religious and social movement reacting to the widespread abandonment of once universally accepted evangelical values: "the
organized determination of conservative churchmen to continue
the imperialistic culture of historic Protestantism within an inhos-
pitable civilization dominated by secular interests and a progressive Christian idealism."[19]

At crucial points in his narrative, Cole evoked the motifs of
rural-urban conflict and cultural obsolescence. Neither was
applied uncritically, though. "Rural," for example, signified mentality more than geography. Though the evidence undeniably
placed them in the major cities of the North, Cole thought that
fundamentalist leaders displayed an outlook distinctively "rural-
minded." The fact that a number of them "were born and raised in
the conservative South" gave traction to his suspicion that fundamentalism was by nature not only antimodern but antiurban too.
Likewise, Cole utilized the cultural lag theme in a nuanced fashion. He identified fundamentalist faith with "antiquated Christian
doctrines" and the "dogmas of mediaeval theology," but fundamentalism, he argued, was not simply the survival of antique
ideas. Cole's greatest achievement was his insight into the psychological process that transformed an ordinary conservative into
an extraordinary fundamentalist. Witnessing the defeat of their
cherished values and the collapse of their once dominant culture,
he said, "conservatives *became* fundamentalists." Adopting psychological jargon then in vogue, Cole diagnosed fundamentalists
as "maladjusted" citizens of a new secular regime.[20]

Throughout the text, Cole struggled with the same problem
of language that would vex fundamentalists and their observers for
many years. At what point does honest description slip into preju-
diced invective? Over the course of some three hundred pages,
Cole repeatedly referred to fundamentalists as extremist, sectarian,
and malcontent "divisionists." He called their piety "uncritical,"
their spirit "censorious," and their social attitudes "perverted." By
contrast, the opponents of the fundamentalists he portrayed as progressive and forward-looking "denominationalists." Like other

early scholars of fundamentalism (and not a few later ones), Cole casually mixed the modes of history and theology.

His groundbreaking work, however, was no ingenuous refutation of fundamentalist claims. While it would hardly satisfy the standards of today's critical historiography, it never sank to the level of antifundamentalist propaganda. Like Mathews, Cole ultimately saw fundamentalism and modernism in creative, dialectical tension. Each movement possessed its own unique charism, and each had untapped potential for historic Christianity. In an era when aging Civil War veterans were laying aside their rancor to seek a national future based on sectional reconciliation, Cole envisioned a new age of religious reconciliation rising out of the ashes of America's most recent culture war. His parting gesture of good will would rarely be matched in the history of fundamentalism studies. "Christianity will reassert its power in the humanly-distraught world," he concluded, "as men nurture the fine sense of religious loyalty that inspired conservatives, as men pioneer with strong heart the unbeaten highways of truth which liberals seek, and as they wed this fervor and discipline into the harmony of Christlike leadership."[21]

Fundamentalism Studies Born Again

In the 1930s, few academic observers shared Cole's vision of a possible marriage between fundamentalist loyalty and modernism's pioneering spirit. Most would have seen the prospects for such a union as incredibly slim. Many academics of the period, as a matter of fact, were thinking more in terms of separation and divorce. The evidence seemed to suggest that American denominations were already engaged in the ecclesiastical equivalent of dividing up the furniture. Earlier the most intellectually gifted of the first-wave fundamentalists, Princeton Seminary's J. Gresham Machen, had advised "the voluntary withdrawal of the liberal ministers" from evangelical churches. Fundamentalists, he wrote in *Christianity and Liberalism* (1923), stood faithful to the confessions upon which the churches were founded. If liberals wished to deny these standards, they were free to leave. "The Unitarian Church," he said, "is frankly and honestly just the kind of church that the liberal preacher desires."[22]

A decade-and-a-half after Machen's book, however, denominational schools and agencies remained firmly in liberal-modernist hands. Even the Southern Baptist Convention, under the leadership of moderate President E. Y. Mullins, had averted a full-scale fundamentalist takeover. Conservatives who, as Cole shrewdly noted, had *become* fundamentalists now counted the cost of becoming separatists and schismatics. In curious imitation of new patterns in modern American romance, modernism kept the house and fundamentalism moved into an efficiency apartment. Machen's own career illustrated this dramatic reversal of fortunes. When he published *Christianity and Liberalism,* he was an ordained Presbyterian minister in good standing and a distinguished, German-trained Ivy League New Testament professor. By the time he died in 1937, he was the defrocked founder of a breakaway seminary and a tiny fundamentalist denomination.[23]

Perhaps even more at odds with Cole's vision of postcontroversy reconciliation was the suspicion that fundamentalism amounted to little more than a spent force. Its double failure in church and culture, clinched by the debacle of the media-hyped *Scopes* trial, convinced many that the movement had run its course. William Warren Sweet spoke of Dayton, Tennessee, as fundamentalism's "last stand."[24] Others buried the phenomenon simply by writing about it in the past tense. The graveyard, not the wedding chapel or divorce court, they supposed, was the proper source of metaphorical material for reflection on the fate of fundamentalism.

Consequently, after Cole's initial venture in fundamentalism studies, the fledgling academic field found it difficult to shake the reputation of irrelevance. Journalistic accounts continued to appear on a frequent basis, as did impressionistic treatments from elite clergy. Novelists, poets, and filmmakers picked up fundamentalism as an enduring motif in the American imagination. But few scholars took the phenomenon seriously enough to risk scarce academic resources on a defunct cultural curiosity.

The Depression-era sea change in academic theology also placed fundamentalism studies in jeopardy. In 1922, at the height of the fundamentalist-modernist controversy, liberal pulpit celebrity Harry Emerson Fosdick threw down the gauntlet with his famous sermon "Shall the Fundamentalists Win?" It indicated the high degree to which analysis of fundamentalism was an integral part of the modernist theological agenda. His 1935 call to go "beyond modernism," however, made it clear that modernism, eclipsed by the rise of Barthian neo-orthodoxy, could no longer offer convincing rationale for further study of its worsted adversary.[25]

Today scholars realize that fundamentalism did not truly vanish after *Scopes;* it just changed its location on the religious landscape. Some say it went underground. Joel Carpenter's *Revive Us Again* (1997) represents the best contemporary scholarship on these hidden years of the movement. Fundamentalism's retreat from mainstream culture, Carpenter has observed, was in reality a strategic redeployment of forces. From the 1930s to the mid-1940s, it took refuge in a largely invisible network of new denominations, educational institutions, publishing houses, and parachurch organizations—a fascinating countercultural matrix that would nurture a new generation of creative leaders.[26] William R. Glass's *Strangers in Zion* (2001) tells how northern-born fundamentalism struggled to establish itself below the Mason-Dixon in the first half of the twentieth century.[27]

During this period, fundamentalism also spread widely throughout the African American evangelical community. *Prophecy* became the watchword for a segment of the black church critical of hot-gospel emotionalism and committed to a more cerebral theological project signified by premillennialism, inerrancy, evangelism, and a propositional model of revelation. According to Oberlin's Albert G. Miller, whose pioneering research has exposed this understudied dimension of the African American religious experience, an "interconnecting network" of conferences, camps, missions agencies, and Bible schools contributed to the construction of a fundamentalist worldview in black denominations between *Scopes* and the civil rights movement. Two key institutions in the network included Atlanta's Carver Bible Institute (later Carver Bible College) and Dallas Colored Bible Institute (now Southern Bible Institute), founded by Edmund Ironside, son of Henry "Harry" Ironside, pastor of Chicago's Moody Church. By the 1960s, the African American fundamentalist tradition had been consolidated in the mission of the National Negro Evangelical Association (later renamed the National Black Evangelical Association).[28]

Ernest Sandeen: Beyond the Modernist Paradigm

The study of fundamentalism entered its own liminal period during the 1930s, waiting for a new crop of scholars to take up the challenge of submitting the movement to critical scrutiny. Just as a reinvented fundamentalism prepared for another engagement with mainstream culture in the 1950s, the academic study of fundamentalism showed new signs of vitality after World War II.

The nationwide revival of religion during the 1950s, coupled with the beginning of Billy Graham's meteoric rise to prominence, convinced a growing number of intellectuals in the academy and the media that fundamentalism had been the victim of a premature obituary. A handful of PhD dissertations produced during the early years of the Cold War approached fundamentalism from new angles of vision. Kenneth Bailey's 1953 Vanderbilt dissertation on the antievolution campaign of the 1920s and Norman F. Furniss's Yale dissertation, published as *The Fundamentalist Controversy, 1918–1931* (1954), supplemented Stewart Cole's work, especially on the topic of evangelical opposition to Darwinism. Louis Gasper's *The Fundamentalist Movement* (1963), based on his Western

Reserve University doctoral work, attempted "to bring the story of fundamentalism up-to-date" by exploring the social and political aspects of the post-*Scopes* subculture. A 1964 Chicago Divinity School dissertation by Roland Nelson investigated the origins of fundamentalism among Northern Baptists.[29] Young church historians, including future leaders in the field Robert Handy and C. C. Goen, contributed fresh interpretations of fundamentalism to scholarly journals.[30] Monographs such as Bailey's *Southern White Protestantism in the Twentieth Century* (1964) and Willard Gatewood's *Preachers, Pedagogues, and Politicians* (1966) set the stage for more empathetic understandings of American conservative religion.[31]

Renewed interest in the *Scopes* trial especially prompted theological and historical reexaminations of fundamentalism's legacy. The Broadway play *Inherit the Wind* (1955) and its 1960 screen adaptation starring Spencer Tracy, Fredric March, and Gene Kelly thrust the "Monkey Trial" center stage in the public imagination. Unfortunately, the uniquely mythic portrayals of the events, informed more by McCarthy-era fears of American fascism than concerns for historical accuracy, reawakened and reinforced distorted images of fundamentalism in mass culture. The Academy Award–winning adaptation of Sinclair Lewis's *Elmer Gantry,* also released in 1960 with an all-star cast, effectively widened the gap between popular interpretations of fundamentalism and emerging academic inquiries into the movement. At the same time, a variety of new books published during this period—including Ray Ginger's *Six Days or Forever?* (1958), Jerry Tompkins's anthology *D-Days at Dayton* (1965), new critical studies of William Jennings Bryan, the autobiography of John Scopes, and Willard Gatewood's sourcebook *Controversy in the Twenties* (1969)—suggested that at least a portion of the academic community and the reading public was ready for more objective and more rigorous investigations into the phenomenon of fundamentalism.[32]

The work most responsible for the rebirth of fundamentalism studies was Ernest R. Sandeen's *The Roots of Fundamentalism: British and American Millenarianism, 1800–1930* (1970).

Educated at Wheaton College and the University of Chicago Divinity School, Sandeen taught history at Macalester College in St. Paul, Minnesota, for several years until his death in 1982. A native of the fundamentalist subculture, he pursued his topic, he admitted, partly as an exercise in self-discovery, or, as he put it, "a quest for historical identity." The genesis of the project, he said, was a conversation with church historian Sidney E. Mead, who suggested that Sandeen critically explore his own tradition's history. Whether or not it brought him the sense of peace that he claimed it did, his work sparked an unexpected renaissance in fundamentalism research. His conclusions are still being debated, but everyone in the field today recognizes Sandeen as the figure who engineered the unanticipated revival of fundamentalism studies and set the agenda for much of the contemporary enterprise.[33]

Sandeen's *Roots of Fundamentalism* ranks as a masterful achievement in intellectual history, highly acclaimed by scholars in a variety of disciplines. A fusion of critical scholarship and empathetic imagination, the book allowed many in the academic world to gain for the first time an insider's view of fundamentalism. In a 1971 review, Calvin College historian George Marsden, who would later make his own mark on the academic study of fundamentalism, called Sandeen's book "the best work on Fundamentalism to date."[34] Since then it has remained a major part of the fundamentalism studies canon.

The Roots of Fundamentalism made four outstanding contributions to the literature on Protestant fundamentalism. First, it acknowledged fundamentalism as primarily religious in nature. It exposed the earlier explanatory hypotheses of cultural lag and rural protest as largely sociological clichés that outran the empirical evidence. It indicted modernist interpretations as unsubstantiated reductionist schemes that sought to explain a genuinely religious movement in terms of nonreligious factors such as economics, geography, class, or psychological defense mechanism. "My aim as a scholar," Sandeen insisted, was to write the history of fundamentalism in such a manner that the "religious vitality and dynamic would not be neglected or subordinated."[35]

Second, the book emphasized the novelty of fundamentalist thought. The documentary data, Sandeen argued, did not support uncritical identification of fundamentalism with *orthodoxy* or *conservatism*. These terms imply continuity with the past, whereas fundamentalism has often been in sharp discontinuity with Christian tradition. Despite the claims of fundamentalists and the charges of their detractors, profound differences separated early fundamentalist theology from Reformation thought and premodern Christian doctrine. Sandeen saw fundamentalism principally as something new — not only a creature of the times but also a surprisingly innovative intellectual movement.

Third, the book put to rest lingering assumptions about the southern character of original fundamentalism. Although previous studies had noted the northern setting of early fundamentalist initiatives, Sandeen effectively demonstrated that southern culture had little impact on the formation of the movement. "No stereotype of the Fundamentalist dies harder than the picture provided by the Scopes trial," he wrote.[36] Urban centers of the northern United States and southern Canada — Boston, New York City, Philadelphia, Detroit, Chicago, Minneapolis, Toronto — were the true birthplaces of the fundamentalist phenomenon. St. Louis, Los Angeles, and Dallas expanded the movement's reach. Dayton, Tennessee, confirmed the pattern by violating it.[37]

Finally, the book maintained that an exclusive focus on the controversies of the 1920s had been responsible for fostering a distorted picture of fundamentalist thought and aspirations. Sandeen accused his predecessors in the field of everything from poor methodology to perpetuating "unsupported operational definitions." "The fate of Fundamentalism in historiography," he despaired, "has been worse than its lot in history."[38] Consequently, much of his work was dedicated to a careful reconstruction of the prehistory of twentieth-century fundamentalism. For Sandeen, the key to fundamentalism studies was the establishment of an accurate definition of fundamentalist identity itself. Clues to the nature of that identity, he believed, lay scattered about in the tracts, sermons, commentaries, hymns, and other writings of a loose confederation of English-speaking evangelical leaders, most of whom lived in the nineteenth century.

Sandeen's evolving thesis added much needed clarity and precision to the study of fundamentalism. In a 1968 pilot project, he defined fundamentalism as the product of an "unstable and incomplete synthesis" of two new nineteenth-century theologies: Anglo-American premillennialism and the doctrine of scriptural inerrancy perfected by Princeton Seminary theologians Charles Hodge, A. A. Hodge, and Benjamin B. Warfield—men who, ironically, eschewed all originality and claimed to teach nothing but "the old Calvinist Theology without modification."[39] By 1970, Sandeen was giving primacy to the eschatological component of that unique theological alliance. He never denied the enormously important role of inerrancy in the formation of the fundamentalist mind. He devoted an entire chapter of *The Roots of Fundamentalism* to its explication and helped a generation of readers distinguish between Princeton's sophisticated notion of inerrancy and the naïve biblical literalism of grassroots American Christianity. But Sandeen's research led him to the conclusion that millennial expectation was the chief ingredient in the fundamentalist mix. "Fundamentalism," he maintained, "ought to be understood partly if not largely as one aspect of the history of millenarianism."[40]

When Sandeen began his research into north Atlantic millenarian thought, eschatology was already a hot topic in the academy. From early twentieth-century biblical studies to the "theologies of hope" that appeared in the 1960s, the theme of eschatology permeated over a half century of theological endeavor. Historians, too, were increasingly captivated by the theme. Norman Cohn's brilliant *Pursuit of the Millennium* (1957) exposed apocalyptic fears and ambitions deep within the Western imagination. Americanists, especially, used eschatology as a lens through which to interpret much of the modern experience. Perry

Miller's reconsideration of the eschatological thrust of the New England Puritan errand, C. C. Goen's rediscovery of Jonathan Edwards's baroque apocalyptic vision, and Ernest Lee Tuveson's reexamination of the American myth of manifest destiny transferred millennial-utopian themes from the periphery of U.S. religious historiography to its center. World War catastrophe and Cold War anxiety primed the American psyche for scholarly reflections on the "end of the world."[41]

As part of this academic turn to the eschatological, Sandeen's history concentrated on what he called the "millenarian" current in Anglo-American Protestant thought. Following Tuveson's *Redeemer Nation* (1968), he used the term *millenarian* to refer to the emerging premillennialist position that emphasized the steady decay of human civilization and the imminent return of Christ. *Millennialist* he reserved for the older postmillennialist doctrine that imagined the sweep of human history as gradual moral improvement culminating in Christ's second advent.

Intriguing and sometimes tragic figures in the millenarian tradition gave Sandeen a prehistory for his fundamentalist movement. His study introduced readers to fascinating characters such as excommunicated Church of Scotland pastor Edward Irving, whose eccentric blend of charismatic and high church teachings gave birth to the Catholic Apostolic Church. Notable Americans in the story included Baptist lay preacher William Miller, whose incorrect calculations for Christ's return in 1843 and 1844 made him a "theological leper" in American history, and onetime treasure hunter Joseph Smith, whose visionary experiences in rural New York's burned-over district led to the founding of the Mormon tradition.[42]

By far, the most important of these figures for Sandeen was John Nelson Darby—not only the chief architect of fundamentalism's future eschatological worldview but also one of the most overlooked creative minds in all of Christian history. Born in 1800, Darby graduated from Trinity College, Dublin, as a Classical Gold Medalist. After a brief stint in law practice, he worked as a parish priest and home missionary in the Church of Ireland until disillusionment with the Anglican establishment cut short his ministerial career. For some fifty years he labored as an itinerate Bible teacher, traveling throughout Europe, North America, and Australia. He was also one of the founding personalities behind the Plymouth Brethren, a loose fellowship of dissenters best known for their rejection of professional ministry, their uncompromising cultural separatism, and their strict adherence to political quietism and ecclesiastical primitivism. A prolific writer and indefatigable controversialist, Darby wrote scores of books and pamphlets, composed hundreds of hymns, and published his own translation of the entire Bible. His letters have been published in three volumes, and his collected writings fill thirty volumes.[43]

Darby's major contribution to nineteenth-century apocalyptic thought came in the form of the eschatological system called dispensational premillennialism. Since the time of Augustine, Christians had been hatching periodization schemes, carving the human adventure into phases (often three or seven) in the attempt to impose upon temporal experience some theologically meaningful shape as it flowed between creation and consummation. Darby's dispensational premillennialism followed this time-honored pattern. An elaborate theology of history based largely on idiosyncratic interpretations of the Books of Daniel and Revelation, it divided the human story into seven "dispensations" or "economies," each distinguished by a different mode of divine government over human affairs—such as conscience, law, or grace. Darby recognized his own age as the sixth and most degenerate stage of the process. The seventh and final period in the scheme he envisioned as the future millennial kingdom.

One of Darby's American disciples, Confederate veteran and former U.S. District Attorney Cyrus I. Scofield, disseminated dispensationalism throughout the evangelical subculture with a popular correspondence course on the Bible and his astonishingly successful *Scofield Reference Bible* (1909). Purporting to reveal the hidden code of sacred writ through its copious notes and

cross-references, the King James Version reference Bible functioned virtually as an evangelical Talmud.[44] At the same time,
evangelists D. L. Moody and Billy Sunday incorporated dispensationalism into the standard repertoire of revivalist pulpit rhetoric. Since the middle of the twentieth century, millions of
evangelicals worldwide have accepted the system as a self-
evident method of "rightly dividing the word of truth" (2 Tim
2:15, KJV). Scofield's student Lewis Sperry Chafer made dispensationalism the cornerstone for his Evangelical Theological College (later Dallas Theological Seminary), and one of Dallas
Seminary's best known professors, Charles Ryrie, packaged dis-
pensationalist hermeneutics for a new generation in his *Ryrie
Study Bible* (1978). Timothy Weber's *Living in the Shadow of
the Second Coming* (1983) still provides the best historical
overview of dispensationalism's incredible legacy.[45]

What made John Nelson Darby truly unique, according to
Sandeen, was not so much his dispensationalism but rather his
distinctive twist on premillennialism. With all other millennialists
and millenarians, Darby assumed that biblical prophecy meant
supernaturally inspired prediction of future events. Like other
premillennialists, he maintained that Christ's second coming
would precede his thousand-year reign on earth. Darby's fierce
defense of eschatological futurism, however, deviated consider-
ably from the contemporary norm. Protestant millenarianism had
traditionally endorsed the opposing view—what is generally
known as eschatological historicism (not to be confused with the
modernist philosophy of the same name). Eschatological histori-
cists, continuing practices patented by medieval Catholic com-
mentators long before them, claimed to find fulfillment of biblical
prophecies in actual historical events (such as the Protestant
Reformation or the French Revolution). By contrast, Darby
believed that biblical prophecies would be fulfilled only in the
future. No event foretold in Revelation, he asserted, would occur
until the return of Christ.

Three novel ideas rooted in this futurist perspective represented for Sandeen the full significance of Darby's dual role as
creative independent thinker and shaper of fundamentalist myth.
The centerpiece of his system—and the unmistakable signature of
subsequent fundamentalist eschatology—was the notion of a
secret, any-time "rapture" of Christians at the moment of Christ's
return. Based on 1 Thessalonians 4:17, which speaks of the saints
being "caught up...in the clouds, to meet the Lord in the air"
(KJV), the teaching became for Darby an article of faith and a test
of fellowship. Eventually, it became a central conceit in fundamentalist film and fiction as well as popular preaching and evangelism. Closely related to the rapture concept was the innovative
doctrine of a two-stage second coming—a secret return "in the air"
to rescue the church, followed by a public and glorious advent to
launch the millennial kingdom. Completing the trio of ideas was
the equally unprecedented conviction that church history functioned as a blank "parenthesis" in God's redemptive plan. Biblical
prophecy, Darby declared, referred only to Israel and the *eschaton,*
not to the pilgrim church on earth. The Christian epic from resurrection to rapture played no role in salvation history.

Sandeen's main concern in *The Roots of Fundamentalism*
was to document the consequences of the rapid spread of Darby's
convictions in the American context. Darby's new eschatological
views gained little foothold in British church life. With the
notable exception of a handful of fellow nonconformists, including George Müller, who ministered to hundreds of industrial-age
orphans exclusively on a faith basis, few Britons paid Darby's
ecclesiastical notions much heed. In the United States, where official disestablishment had already given sectarianism free rein,
Darby's ecclesiology made even less impact. His apocalyptic system, however, struck a sensitive nerve. Nineteenth-century America, Sandeen noted, was "drunk on the millennium,"[46] and
Darby's radical vision only fed the national addiction.

From the 1870s to the early twentieth century, Darby's ideas
were transmitted to a diverse group of Reformed and Wesleyan

Protestant leaders in the Northeast and Midwest through a series of popular Bible and prophecy conferences cutting across denominational lines. This network of parachurch institutions and the unique kind of ecumenism that it fostered created a community primed to push American evangelicalism toward its next phase of evolution. As an ascending modernism forced conservative evangelical authorities increasingly into defensive positions, Darby's unconventional eschatology unexpectedly surfaced as the standard of the orthodoxy they rallied to defend.

For erstwhile fundamentalist Sandeen, Darbyite millenarianism represented the heart of the early fundamentalist movement. A unique convergence of historical forces formed fundamentalism out of the clay of transatlantic revivalism and reactive antimodernism. Princeton's error-free Bible gave it skeletal structure. Effective animation, however, came from the most recent innovation in Christianity's never-ending obsession with last things. As Sandeen saw it, Darby breathed into the nostrils of a threatened late Victorian evangelicalism, and fundamentalism became a living soul. The era of modernist dominance in fundamentalism studies was over.

3
The Varieties of Protestant Fundamentalism Studies

The publication of Ernest Sandeen's *Roots of Fundamentalism* in 1970 coincided with a key phase of Protestant fundamentalism's surprising resurgence in American culture. Far from a requiem for the movement, the book testified to fundamentalism's stunning resilience and lively career. The second edition of the book appeared in 1978. By then, a reinvigorated, and to some extent reinvented, fundamentalism was fast becoming a fixture of American life—influencing everything from entertainment and corporate culture to politics and public education. As early as the 1950s, some observers were speaking of a neo-fundamentalist renaissance. By the late 1970s, pundits were tracking a related phenomenon called the New Religious Right.

This chapter addresses an issue in fundamentalism studies that became increasingly important after the post–World War II revival of Protestant fundamentalism: methodology. What is the most effective way to study fundamentalism? If fundamentalism is principally a set of ideas or a worldview, how can that mindset be properly investigated? If fundamentalism constitutes a collection of cultural practices, how can those patterns best be recognized and examined?

As we have seen, the first scholars to submit fundamentalism to academic scrutiny were Christian theologians writing from a modernist perspective. The scholars who established fundamentalism studies as a distinct field in the 1970s and 1980s were professional historians intent on abandoning the modernist theological paradigm. Since that time, academics in a number of other disciplines have contributed to the growing body of research on the subject utilizing diverse and creative methodologies.

A few self-declared fundamentalists have contributed to the field. George W. Dollar, longtime church historian at Bob Jones University (BJU), and Ed Dobson and Ed Hindson, both associated with Jerry Falwell's Liberty University, attempted to produce narrative and analytical accounts of fundamentalism accessible to insider and outsider audiences during the 1970s and 1980s. More recently, Jim Owen, historian at The Master's College in California, has offered a defense of fundamentalism's social record from the critical years of the Great Depression and World War II.[1] Arguably the best history of fundamentalism from an insider's point of view is *In Pursuit of Purity: American Fundamentalism Since 1850* (1986) by David O. Beale, Dollar's successor at BJU. Relatively free from apologetic animus, the book is notable for its frank portrayal of fundamentalist ambivalence before the alternatives of worldly success and spiritual integrity. Paul's exhortation to "come out from among them and be ye separate" (2 Cor 6:17, KJV), Beale has explained, has been heeded in various ways by fundamentalists in the American context.[2]

For good or for ill, Beale's work has made little impact on the academic study of fundamentalism. It represents an in-house treatment of fundamentalism designed to bolster the self-understanding of critical minds within the subculture. The chief architects of academic fundamentalism studies in the last few decades, instead, have come from circles far from Beale's. Since Sandeen, virtually all scholars in the field of Protestant fundamentalism research have been former fundamentalists, moderate to "lapsed" evangelicals, or individuals unaffiliated with the evangelical tradition altogether.

This chapter explores the developments in historical studies, feminist studies, and ethnographic analysis produced by these mainstream academics. Their scholarship, shaped largely by the changing character of the discipline of religious studies, greatly expanded and enriched the field of fundamentalism studies after the 1970s. In this chapter, we focus on the work of three representative figures: George Marsden, Betty DeBerg, and Brenda Brasher.

Fundamentalism Redux

First, however, we should briefly review the unanticipated reappearance of Protestant fundamentalism in the American experience. The revival of fundamentalism, stretching from the late 1940s to the early 1980s, constituted a significant part of a large-scale turnabout in U.S. religious life after World War II. Earlier in the century, prophecies of secularization had predicted the eventual diminishment or even disappearance of religion in society. Based on a mixture of empirical evidence and Enlightenment bias, these theories claimed that the dynamics of modern life, especially science, would push religion to the edges of social existence and intellectual relevance. Such marginalized religion would be only a shadow of its former self. The stripping of the public square during the 1960s, which included the removal of God-talk and religious symbols from the public school classroom, seemed to indicate that America was indeed on the verge of a new postreligious era. Fashionable quests for "religionless" Christianity in the theological establishment also lent validity to the secularization thesis.

At the same time, evidence of other sorts suggested that the United States was still Chesterton's "nation with the soul of a church." The wave of secularization produced an undertow of spiritual yearning. The religious revival of the 1950s had bumped religious affiliation and attendance rates to new heights. Billy Graham's ascent to the role of unofficial national chaplain registered enduring public respect for religion. Robert Bellah's research into civil religion exposed deep-seated spiritual motives operating outside conventional religious channels. Survey data regarding belief in God and life after death continued to identify the United States as the most religious country in the industrialized West.

In addition, religious pluralism, always a defining element of grassroots American culture, became much more visible and extensive during this period. The Zen boom, the Jesus freak movement, the religious rhetoric of the civil rights movement, and the appeal of new "alternative altars" in the emerging youth culture and the decaying inner cities demonstrated that America was just as religiously fertile as ever. On the individual level, Americans transgressed traditional confessional boundaries in ways never before imaginable. Many experimented with customized ventures in religious dual citizenship or hyphenated religious identity. In the public realm, the elimination of federal immigration quotas during the Johnson administration effectively turned "one nation under God" into a multicultural nation under a pantheon of diverse deities.[3]

In the late 1960s and early 1970s, some of the country's most insightful scholars of religion scrambled to account for the persistence and fecundity of religion in American culture. Harvard theologian Harvey Cox, whose 1965 classic *The Secular City* had celebrated the advent of postreligious technopolis, tempered his enthusiasm for Apollonian secularity with explorations of Dionysian fantasy and mysticism in *The Feast of Fools* (1969) and *The Seduction of the Spirit* (1973). Sociologist Peter Berger openly questioned secularization theory in *Rumors of Angels* (1969) and *The Heretical Imperative* (1979). Fellow social scientist Andrew Greeley aired his second thoughts in *Unsecular Man* (1972). By the end of the 1970s, historian William McLoughlin went on record with an intriguing countertheory to secularization. According to his calculations, America was experiencing nothing less than another in a series of "great awakenings."[4]

Martin Marty summarized the trend toward reassessment this way. The concept of secularization corresponded to genuine shifts of loyalty and perception in modern society, he observed, but it did not accurately track the migrations of the holy in late twentieth-century America. Nor did it adequately appreciate what appeared to be the incurably religious nature of the American people. "Religion was not disappearing," he said, "it was relocating."[5]

American Catholics experienced that relocation of religion during the period of Vatican II (1962–65), when official reforms and unauthorized experiments in public ritual and private piety dramatically altered Catholic sacramental life. Massive defections from the priesthood and the convent transfigured Catholic institutional life, as rising levels of private and public dissent from Church teaching brought older notions of Catholic identity and self-consciousness into question. Combined with general social forces such as suburbanization and increasing rates of mobility, these developments effectively closed the era of American "ghetto" Catholicism that had seemed so permanent to both Catholic and non-Catholic alike. Arguably the developments also laid the foundation for the creation of new, distinctively Catholic, forms of fundamentalism—an issue we take up in the following chapter.

Another major part of the post–World War II relocation of religion, intimately related to the reappearance of evangelical fundamentalism, was a transformation of the status of mainline Protestantism. Named after the streetcar line that ran through Philadelphia's elite suburban neighborhoods, mainline Protestantism represented those historic denominations that had enjoyed great institutional prosperity for nearly a century after the Civil War. Culturally influential, organizationally complex, intellectually respectable, and overwhelmingly white in membership, the mainline churches were those denominations securely aligned with the liberal/neo-orthodox theological legacy, the social gospel agenda, and the new mission of ecumenical dialogue. Northern and midwestern cities provided a demographic base for the American mainline. The National Council of Churches (NCC) gave it a nationwide framework. *Christian Century, Guideposts,* and the Revised Standard Version of the Bible expressed its multidimensional ethos in print. Union Seminary's Reinhold Niebuhr and positive-thinking Norman Vincent Peale personified respectively the hard and soft sides of its intellectual life. The Interchurch Center on Manhattan's Upper West Side—known colloquially as "The God Box"—was the concrete symbol of the mainline's institutional success and presumed permanence. Millions of middle-class, college-educated Episcopalians, Presbyterians, Congregationalists, Methodists, Lutherans, Disciples of Christ, and Northern (later American) Baptists constituted its faithful rank and file. Through regular attendance and record-breaking financial giving, they made the 1950s and early 1960s the heyday of mainline Protestantism.[6]

The shock of the 1970s, however, was the realization that the mainline "golden age" was over. Just as America seemed most open to the progressive, inclusive message of the liberal churches, mainline Protestantism entered a period of steep institutional decline. The numbers told the story in graphic detail. From 1970 to the late 1990s, as the U.S. population grew by over 30 percent, the United Methodist Church, the Episcopal Church, the Presbyterian Church (U.S.A.), and other mainline bodies lost more members than they gained. By the early twenty-first century, Muslims in America outnumbered Episcopalians and nearly matched United Methodists. The number of Buddhists in the United States exceeded that of American Baptists. America's Hindu population rivaled that of the United Church of Christ.[7]

The real threat to the mainline denominations, however, came from sources much closer to home. *Why Conservative Churches Are Growing* (1972) by NCC executive Dean Kelley identified the trend for decades to come. Robert Wuthnow's *Restructuring of American Religion* (1988) confirmed Kelley's controversial thesis. Though certain sectors of American society had been profoundly secularized in the years following World War II, most Americans continued to see themselves as religious in one way or another. The vast majority of religious Americans associated Christianity with cultural and political conservatism. Traditional denominational identity was eroding, and top-heavy mainline institutions were veering dangerously toward irrelevance. Groups that preached an exclusive, countercultural creed and made high demands on the time and treasure of their members, however, were growing by leaps and bounds. The statistical winners of the late twentieth century were those groups positioned to varying degrees outside the cultural mainstream: Southern Baptists, Pentecostals, Mormons, and non-denominational Christians. In *The Churching of America* (1992), sociologists Roger Finke and Rodney Stark articulated what amounted to the law of natural selection in the American religious jungle: *"religious organizations are stronger to the degree that they impose significant costs in terms of sacrifice and even stigma upon their members."*[8]

No strangers to sacrifice or stigma, fundamentalists of the 1970s and early 1980s took advantage of their newfound strength in myriad ways. Educators among the new generation of fundamentalists refurbished academic institutions that had survived the lean years of cultural exile after *Scopes,* capitalizing on a well-cultivated sense of alternative identity and mission. Writers and editors in the thriving subculture published runaway bestsellers on everything from self-help to creation science and Armageddon. Artists in the movement created innovative entertainment enclaves, producing both the low-budget apocalyptic thrillers that aped Hollywood science fiction and the Christian rock phenomenon that mimicked popular music and revolutionized evangelical worship. Enterprising entrepreneurs established target niches in the American marketplace, developing goods and services specifically tailored to the young and worldly evangelical consumers of the era.[9] Church growth gurus turned the art of soul-winning into a science, and pastoral executives introduced the mega-church into the religious environment. Electronic church pioneers built media empires that have since earned a permanent place in American folklore.

Those best poised to profit from fundamentalism's upgraded status were conservative Protestants who sailed under the colors of "new evangelicalism." Popularized by Boston pastor and J. Gresham Machen protégé Harold John Ockenga, the term was intended to indicate fundamentalist theology in a new key—a reformed fundamentalism invigorated with a "spirit of cooperation, of mutual faith, of progressive action, and of ethical responsibility."[10] The neo-evangelicals sought to combine unyielding commitment to the fundamentals of biblical inerrancy and theistic supernaturalism with a more irenic attitude toward Christians of other persuasions and a heightened sense of obligation to engage culture directly. They were especially interested in shedding the Elmer Gantry image acquired, rightly or wrongly, by traditional fundamentalism. *Christianity Today* magazine, conceived by Billy Graham and underwritten by Sun Oil tycoon J. Howard Pew, took neo-evangelicalism's conservative yet upbeat message to the American middle. The National Association of Evangelicals (NAE) provided broad-based infrastructure. Institutions such as Fuller Theological Seminary in California, brainchild of radio evangelist Charles E. Fuller, and the Evangelical Theological Society advanced the movement's ambition for intellectual respectability. Parachurch organizations such as Youth for Christ, Inter-Varsity Christian Fellowship, Fellowship of Christian Athletes, Campus Crusade for Christ, and the Navigators infused the movement with clean-cut idealism.

Not every quarter of the fundamentalist community benefited from religious America's postwar turn to the right, however. Some self-styled fundamentalists condemned neo-evangelicalism's mission to the mainstream and squandered any claim to cultural relevance in the process. From their perspective, Billy Graham's "cooperative evangelism" and Jerry Falwell's conservative coalition across confessional lines violated the cardinal tenet of ecclesiastical separatism. In the words of the apostle Paul, they said, Graham and Falwell had become "unequally yoked together with unbelievers" (2 Cor 6:14, KJV)—the unforgivable sin of fundamentalism. What the far-right intransigents could not argue with, however, was the apparent success of such innovative initiatives. Stalwarts such as the Bob Joneses of BJU, the "World's Most Unusual University," and John R. Rice, editor of *Sword of the Lord* and author of *Bobbed Hair, Bossy Wives, and Women Preachers* (1941), eventually found themselves on the sidelines of American religion's newest growth industry.

Pentecostals, on the other hand, soared on the coattails of their neo-fundamentalist and neo-evangelical kin. A product of the same cultural matrix that gave rise to original fundamentalism, Pentecostalism shared the more doctrinally oriented movement's forebodings about American secularization and its sense of urgency regarding Christian mission in the latter-days of history. Theologically the two movements overlapped on a number of other key issues, too, including biblical authority, personal piety, creationism, the exclusivity of salvation through Christ, and the imminent return of the Lord like "a thief in the night" (1 Thess 5:2, KJV). Pentecostalism's distinctive emphasis upon Spirit baptism and the modern legitimacy of supernatural spiritual gifts set it apart from classical fundamentalism, which followed Reformation precedent in assigning miracles to a distant biblical past. Pentecostalism also had a more progressive record on race and gender. Increasingly, historians are emphasizing the black roots of the movement and its historic openness to female ministry. Recent studies have attempted to reconstruct the still largely untold stories of Apostolic Faith pastor William J. Seymour, leader of the famous Azusa Street Revival in Los Angeles (1906–9), a host of innovative African American organizers in the holiness community, and scores of women preachers, teachers, missionaries, writers, and editors now nearly lost to history.[11] At the midpoint of the twentieth century, however, both Pentecostalism and fundamentalism struggled to overcome derogatory stereotypes of "holy-rollers" and "Bible-thumpers" still strong in American prejudice.

After Oral Roberts's breakthrough in primetime broadcasting during the 1960s and the contemporaneous unleashing of charismatic renewal in mainline and liturgical circles, things dramatically changed. Thanks to tongues-speaking Episcopal priest Dennis Bennett, California dairyman Demos Shakarian's Full Gospel Business Men's Fellowship International, the ecumenically minded "Mr. Pentecost" David du Plessis, and a generation of Spirit-filled midwestern Catholic college students, Pentecostal fervor moved from the backwoods of Dust Bowl desperation to the boardrooms of corporate America, the locker rooms of professional sports teams, and the living rooms of the nation's leisure class. What had once been dismissed as the fire-baptized vision of disinherited rural nobodies became the chic spirituality of choice for some of the best and brightest in suburban America. Like the second coming of fundamentalism, the mainstreaming of Pentecostalism became one of the surprising stories of modern religious history. By 2000, over 70 million Americans—500 million people worldwide—identified their Christianity as Pentecostal or charismatic.[12]

Perhaps the greatest measure of conservative Protestantism's success in the wake of the mainline's collapse was its impact on American politics, especially the changing profile of the U.S. presidency. With few exceptions, the mainline establishment had been custodian of presidential spirituality from Washington to Truman. Billy Graham's baptism of President Eisenhower—literally in the White House—symbolized (albeit privately) an important moment of transition. After John F. Kennedy decisively broke the mainline Protestant lock on the White House, outsider fundamentalism increasingly gained access to the country's ultimate insider position. Richard Nixon's friendship with Billy Graham legitimized conservative evangelicalism in the eyes of the Vietnam-era, middle-class "silent majority." Jimmy Carter's post-Watergate, born-again populism made non-mainline religion front-page news during the bicentennial "Year of the Evangelical." Ronald Reagan's phenomenal success, due in part to the efforts of Jerry Falwell's Moral Majority, James Robison's Religious Roundtable, and a broad coalition of other "Christian soldiers" associated with the New Religious Right, made it clear that a startlingly new pattern of influence was emerging in U.S. religion. Pat Robertson's bid for the Republican nomination drove home the indisputable fact. By the 1980s, religious communities outside the old liberal mainstream were now the principal sources of America's leadership class. Faith-healers and televangelists were the new king makers in postsecular America.[13]

Historical Studies: George Marsden

During the 1980s, American academics eager to come to terms with the incredible perseverance of fundamentalism and the elusive quality of the secularization process found Ernest Sandeen's explanation of fundamentalism only partially satisfying. The roots of fundamentalism may have been in Anglo-American millennialism and Princeton inerrancy, but the fruits of resurgent fundamentalism were undeniably this-worldly and extrabiblical. Eschatological and supernaturalist themes still held sway over the fundamentalist imagination. Hal Lindsey's *Late Great Planet Earth* (1970), the runaway bestseller of the 1970s, proved as much. Harold Lindsell's confrontational *Battle for the Bible* (1976) showed that affirmation of biblical infallibility remained the litmus test for fundamentalist purity. The rhetoric and public actions of self-proclaimed fundamentalist Jerry Falwell and his many imitators, however, were stridently political, even partisan. An activist agenda promoting fiscal conservatism, creation science, military superiority, and a "Christian" America—not to mention antifeminist, antiabortion, and antigay agitation—was hard to square with the millennial quietism of John Darby's other-worldly dispensationalism and the ivory-tower intellectualism of Princeton's Charles Hodge. Fundamentalists still gave lip service to Christ's any-time return and the doctrinal intricacies of inerrancy, but their media blitzes, direct-mail campaigns, fundraising efforts, and voter registration drives concentrated on the more mundane affair of an escalating culture war in America.

Oxford University Press released George M. Marsden's *Fundamentalism and American Culture* (1980) just in time for American readers to make sense of the astonishing events reshaping their world. Though focused on the emergent generations of American fundamentalists, much as Sandeen's work had been, Marsden's intentionally revisionist approach to fundamentalism allowed readers to gain even greater insight into what was evidently an unfinished force in American experience. Soon after its publication, *Fundamentalism and American Culture* superseded *The Roots of Fundamentalism* as the standard text on the subject. Fellow academics quickly came to regard Marsden as the leading authority on Protestant fundamentalism in the United States.

Marsden's background and education uniquely qualified him to be an effective interpreter of Protestant fundamentalism during the years of its reawakening.[14] His father was a minister in Machen's Orthodox Presbyterian Church, whose circle of friends included Carl McIntire, founder of the anti-NCC American Council of Churches, and Harold Ockenga, first president of the NAE and founding president of Fuller Seminary. After taking a BA degree at Haverford College, Marsden studied at Westminster Theological Seminary and then at Yale with historian of American religion Sydney Ahlstrom and Puritanism expert Edmund Morgan in the American studies doctoral program. He taught history at Michigan's Calvin College for over two decades before moving to the American church history post at Duke Divinity School. In 1992, he accepted the Francis A. McAnaney chair in history at the University of Notre Dame.

Though trained as a historian, Marsden has never minimized his evangelical credentials or his theological interests. Reformed apologist Cornelius Van Til, Dutch Calvinist Abraham Kuyper, fundamentalist philosopher Francis A. Schaeffer, and neo-orthodox theologian Reinhold Niebuhr especially influenced his religious vision. Theologically he should be placed in the context of the general reassessment of the fundamentalist legacy conducted by moderate evangelicals during the second half of the twentieth century. Carl F. H. Henry, founding editor of *Christianity Today* and dean of evangelical theologians until his death in 2003, is usually credited with initiating the reevaluation. The secular media called him "the thinking man's Billy Graham." In *The Uneasy Conscience of Modern Fundamentalism* (1947), his manifesto for the new evangelicalism, Henry challenged conservative evangelicals to discard fundamentalism's negativity and "social impotence" and apply the "genius" of their position to the problems of modern culture in a positive way.[15] Henry's younger contemporary Edward John Carnell, Fuller professor and president, articulated the same argument more forcefully in *The Case for Orthodox Theology* (1959). Defining *fundamentalism* as *"orthodoxy gone cultic,"* he drew a sharp distinction between a full-bodied evangelical Christianity rooted in historic orthodoxy and a fundamentalism cut off from "the wisdom of the ages."[16] Marsden's fellow evangelical historian Mark Noll offered what many consider to be the definitive critique in this vein. In *The Scandal of the Evangelical Mind* (1994), he praised fundamentalism for its defense of revealed religion in an age of one-dimensional positivism but blamed the "intellectual disaster" of fundamentalism on its indefensible attempt to make the "worst features" of nineteenth-century intellectual culture the "methodological keystones" for contemporary Christian thought.[17]

Like Noll, Marsden has also shown a keen interest in separating the gold of authentic evangelical Christianity from the dross of the "culturally formed assumptions, ideals, and values" that, in his judgment, severely circumscribed early fundamentalism's effectiveness in culture. Such a task, he has argued, is incumbent upon the "Christian historian" in all aspects of his or her vocation—a calling that includes distinguishing "God's genuine work from practices that have no greater authority than the customs or ways of thinking of a particular time and place."[18] Much of Marsden's work, in fact, has betrayed a preoccupation with the challenge of doing history from such a self-consciously Christian perspective. His publications of the 1990s gave expression to a particular concern for the unique role of a Christian voice in higher education: *The Secularization of the Academy* (1992), *The Soul of the American University* (1994), and *The Outrageous Idea of Christian Scholarship* (1997).[19] Some critics see his *Jonathan Edwards: A Life* (2003), both a chronicle and a celebration of "rigorous God-centeredness in the modern era,"[20] as the crowning achievement of a career devoted to the ideal of Christian scholarship.

Marsden's contribution to fundamentalism scholarship, however, will most likely define his legacy in the study of American religion. In addition to *Fundamentalism and American Culture,* his major publications in the field include *Reforming Fundamentalism: Fuller Seminary and the New Evangelicalism* (1987), a collection of essays entitled *Understanding Fundamentalism and Evangelicalism* (1991), and numerous journal articles and book chapters. His articles on fundamentalism in Mircea Eliade's *Encyclopedia of Religion* (1986) and the *Encyclopedia of the American Religious Experience* (1988) have virtually guaranteed his influence on the future of fundamentalism studies.[21]

Fundamentalism and American Culture, now in its second edition, remains Marsden's most comprehensive treatment of the dynamics of fundamentalism. Framed in part as a corrective to Sandeen, the book was designed to be a "dispassionate analysis of the development of a significant Christian tradition in an American cultural setting." Like Sandeen, Marsden rejected the reductionist schemes of the past that denied the religious and intellectual integrity of fundamentalism. He also approached his subject with much the same respect and empathy that Sandeen had manifested in his pioneering work. The distinctiveness of Marsden's work was its broader interpretive grasp, its call for a reexamination of the "wider roots" of the fundamentalist movement.[22]

Marsden differed with Sandeen on the basic question of fundamentalism's constitutional makeup. He maintained that

Sandeen's definition of fundamentalism as a synthesis of dispensational premillennialism and Princeton inerrancy too narrowly pictured the movement as a purely doctrinal innovation. Though Marsden tackled fundamentalism primarily as a problem in intellectual history, he criticized Sandeen for minimizing the impact of cultural issues. As he saw it, Sandeen's monograph did not take stock of the full range of factors informing the fundamentalist movement, nor did it penetrate to the level of the movement's ideology or worldview.

Marsden's debate with Sandeen first surfaced in the pages of the *Christian Scholar's Review* during the early 1970s, when Marsden was associate editor of the journal. In that context, he suggested that Sandeen's work disproportionately featured two out of several components in the fundamentalist matrix. He especially objected to the identification of millenarianism as fundamentalism's "organizing principle." Factors such as antiliberalism, antievolution, missionary enthusiasm, ecclesiastical separatism, and moral purity, he argued, played equally important parts in the formation of fundamentalism. Millennialism, moreover, did not apply universally (J. Gresham Machen's opposition to premillennialism being a case in point). Rendering his alternative view with algebraic precision, Marsden put other elements (p, q, r, etc.) on equal footing with millennialism (m) and proposed "antiworldliness" (w) as the common denominator:

$$\text{Fund.} = \frac{m + p + q + r \text{ etc.}}{w}$$

"Since this formula contains a variety of separable elements," he concluded, "I contend that in order to trace the roots of Fundamentalism it is necessary to trace the roots of each of these elements."[23]

Fundamentalism and American Culture attempted to do just that. By 1980, though, Marsden's understanding of fundamentalism as a multidimensional reality had matured significantly beyond the working hypotheses articulated in intramural competition with Sandeen. A decade of research into the movement's dependence upon common sense realism, as well as its appropriation of nineteenth-century notions of holiness and longstanding ideals of Christian civilization, had led Marsden to conclude that fundamentalism could best be understood as "a sub-species of American revivalism rather than as an outgrowth of the movements espousing millenarianism or inerrancy."[24] His lasting achievement in *Fundamentalism and American Culture* was the creation of a richly nuanced portrait of the fundamentalist movement that captured the lucidity of its early modern mental world, the vigor of its late Victorian moral imagination, the complexity of its internal composition, and the unmistakably American character of its cultural embodiment. After Marsden, critics could indict fundamentalists for unfashionable beliefs and values, but no one could credibly accuse them of philosophical naivete, endorsement of premodern cosmology, or retreat from the challenges of culture.

Further reflection on the question of fundamentalism's organizing principle also forced Marsden to abandon his earlier speculation about antiworldliness as the common denominator undergirding the movement's diverse experiments in theological and cultural reform. With increasing intensity his publications emphasized antimodernist militancy as the salient feature of fundamentalist experience. The sine qua non for fundamentalism, he came to believe, was an acute sense of crisis—the alarming conviction that certain core aspects of the modernization process placed the essence of Christian life and thought in dire jeopardy. Borrowing categories from Thomas Kuhn's influential book *The Structure of Scientific Revolutions* (1962), Marsden located the genesis of the fundamentalist project in the trauma of an unexpected "paradigm conflict,"[25] as competing models of knowledge, religion, and morality struggled to dominate twentieth-century America.

Marsden's definition of a *fundamentalist* as "an evangelical who is angry about something"[26] may well outlive the debates sparked by his more technical arguments. Shorthand characterizations of fundamentalism such as Clark Pinnock's "evangelicalism under pressure" and Karen Armstrong's "embattled faith"[27] owe much of their classroom utility to Marsden's painstaking research in the primary sources of American fundamentalism. Linking fundamentalist anger and anxiety to the centrifugal force of secular modernity, Marsden brought new clarity to the academic study of fundamentalism. Consensus in the field today recognizes antimodern or countermodern protest as the working definition of fundamentalism.

Feminist Studies: Betty DeBerg

George Marsden refocused fundamentalism scholarship at the moment when, according to Jerry Falwell, American Protestant fundamentalism had "come of age."[28] Media coverage of the New Religious Right made fundamentalism a household word. So did the "Gospelgate" scandals involving prominent televangelists Jim Bakker, Oral Roberts, and Jimmy Swaggart. With the widespread application of the *fundamentalism* label to movements of religious militancy in the Islamic world, especially revolutionary Iran, Marsden's work gained new global relevance. The study of fundamentalism seemed to be targeting some of the most vibrant religious forces on the planet.

At the same time, Marsden's own discipline was undergoing a season of substantial change that would greatly affect the study of fundamentalism. What was traditionally known as American *church* history was rapidly giving way to American *religious* history. Young scholars in the field sought to recover the religious past of the American experience without reference to the touchstones of theological, denominational, and ethnocentric bias that had defined the seminary-centered enterprise since the nineteenth century. Endeavoring to jettison what R. Laurence Moore called the Protestant establishment's "historiography of desire,"[29] the new historians of U.S. religion, increasingly affiliated with state university religious studies departments, cobbled together interdisciplinary methodologies that reflected the contemporary ferment in literary criticism, American studies, and the social sciences. They also measured their work by the same academic standards that governed research in more secular areas of history. In so far as Marsden grounded his project in "a Christian view of history," marked by talk of God's action in the world,[30] he resisted the new directions in American religious history.

One important dimension of the new American religious history was a keen interest in women's history. Since the 1848 Seneca Falls Woman's Rights Convention, the women's movement in the United States had stimulated scholarship investigating female roles in religious organizations, images of women in official doctrine and authoritative texts, and the unexamined world of women's spiritual experience. *The Woman's Bible* (1895–98), a collaborative commentary project inspired and coordinated by Elizabeth Cady Stanton, initiated a current of literature that mixed philosophical critique with historical inquiry into the "invisible" past of American women. During the 1970s, a spate of publications—many now classics—submitted the American religious experience to new feminist scrutiny. Amanda Porterfield's *Feminine Spirituality in America* (1970), Barbara Welter's *Dimity Convictions* (1976), Nancy Cott's *The Bonds of Womanhood* (1977), and Ann Douglas's *The Feminization of American Culture* (1977) revolutionized a field once exclusively focused on the ideas and institutions of male clergy.

In the decade following Marsden's *Fundamentalism and American Culture,* a number of scholars employed these fresh interpretive strategies in the quest for even greater insight into fundamentalist belief and practice. Timothy Weber, a student of Martin Marty, updated and enlarged his history of American premillennialism. *Living in the Shadow of the Second Coming* (1983, 1987) took an unprecedented behavioral approach to fundamentalism's most recognizable teaching. Laurence Moore, who like Marsden trained with Ahlstrom at Yale, and Kathleen C. Boone, one of the few English literature PhDs in fundamentalism studies, exemplified the current fascination with then avant-garde deconstruction criticism as they attempted to expose the heterogeneity of fundamentalism's texts. Betraying the influence of Jacques Derrida, Moore's essay on "The Protestant Majority as a Lost Generation" in *Religious Outsiders and the Making of Americans* (1986) explored the polysemous and ironic character of fundamentalism's signature outsider rhetoric.[31] Boone's *The Bible Tells Them So* (1989), drawing upon Michel Foucault's poststructuralism and Stanley Fish's reader-response theory, represented the first serious analysis of an inerrant Bible's authority in the "*verbal* system" of fundamentalist discourse.[32]

Arguably the best study of fundamentalism from a feminist angle during this period was Betty DeBerg's *Ungodly Women* (1990). An expanded version of her Vanderbilt doctoral dissertation, this history of first-wave fundamentalism reopened the old question of fundamentalism's essential nature. Upon its release, DeBerg emerged as a trendsetter in the study of conservative evangelical Christianity. Margaret Lamberts Bendroth's *Fundamentalism and Gender* (1994), R. Marie Griffith's *God's Daughters* (1997), and a number of other studies published in the 1990s and early twenty-first century confirmed DeBerg's claim that she had struck a rich vein in fundamentalism studies.[33] Over the course of a career that has taken her from the theology department at Valparaiso University to the philosophy and religion department at the University of Northern Iowa, DeBerg has published on subjects ranging from women in North American Lutheranism to the practice and study of religion in U.S. higher education.[34] *Ungodly Women,* however, continues to be her best-known and most influential work.

DeBerg's chief aim in *Ungodly Women* was to advance the research on fundamentalism by addressing a perceived gap in the growing critical literature. She reassessed nearly six decades of scholarly work on fundamentalism and found both recent interpretations and earlier, allegedly reductionist, treatments significantly flawed. The cultural lag and rural-urban hypotheses outran the evidence, she argued, while Sandeen and Marsden, though justified in their emphasis on the religious nature of fundamentalism, overlooked the deep cultural loyalties embedded in the doctrine and devotion. Neither the cultural nor the theological interpretative model, she wrote, "has been adequate to explain fully the origins and nature of American fundamentalism."[35]

What was missing in previous efforts to comprehend fundamentalism, DeBerg claimed, was frank recognition of the presence of gender ideology in early fundamentalist discourse. Marsden had charged Sandeen with neglecting fundamentalism's investment in culture, especially the assumptions animating late Victorian America. DeBerg indicted Marsden for failing to go far enough in his reevaluation of fundamentalism's cultural dimension. Theology, understood in the traditional sense of rational discourse about God, scripture, and religious ideas, remained the prime concern. Sex was a huge blind spot. *The Roots of Fundamentalism* and *Fundamentalism and American Culture* contained only a handful of women's names and even fewer references to women, gender, or feminism as relevant topics. By contrast, DeBerg discovered women—or, more properly, the topic of women—to be nearly ubiquitous in the "rhetorical substructure" of fundamentalist thought. "Matters related to human sexual identity and behavior," she declared, "occupied a central place in fundamentalists' moral and religious teaching."[36]

DeBerg supported her thesis with evidence culled from the popular religious press of early fundamentalism. Dissatisfied with Sandeen's and Marsden's uncritical focus on the official fundamentalism of seminary founders, celebrity pastors, and denominational leaders, she sought to reconstruct the worldview of vernacular Protestant fundamentalism in the movement's formative period. Her research method involved content analysis of sermons and speeches delivered to large lay audiences and periodic literature geared to general readers. In publications such as Curtis Lee Laws's *Watchman-Examiner,* the *King's Business* of the Bible Institute of Los Angeles, and *Moody Bible Institute Monthly,* DeBerg encountered a new American religious coalition not only nervous about its loss of cultural prestige and the erosion of belief in the supernatural but also profoundly disturbed by a vast sea change in gender roles and family life.

DeBerg couched her history of the fundamentalist imagination in the broader narrative of shifting attitudes toward gender differentiation in American culture. Prior to *Ungodly Women,* groundbreaking work in the field of women's studies had identified a series of revolutions in American manners and morals — from the breakdown of Puritanism's patriarchal family and the canonization of the Victorian cult of true womanhood to the rise of the sexually independent flapper of the 1920s. Each revolution inaugurated a sweeping transformation of American life. Each called into question time-honored patterns of courtship, marriage, child rearing, health care, entertainment, and personal expression.

The record of disparate American reactions to this legacy of social change is today a standard part of U.S. social historiography. DeBerg was the first scholar to make the case that fundamentalism was directly linked to that heritage. As the New Woman of the late nineteenth century gave way to the suffragette and lost-generation flapper, conservative evangelicals, especially members of the urban bourgeoisie, attempted to define their distinctive cultural identity over against the new sexual mores. Some high-profile evangelicals, such as Billy Sunday and William Jennings Bryan, publicly advocated the political enfranchisement of women, but most evangelicals distinguished between legitimate civic rights and what they considered to be unwarranted departures from traditional, even biblical, moral standards. A faction of the evangelical community responded to these seismic shifts in values and behavior by launching a nostalgic attempt to retrieve at least portions of the Victorian ideal and a zealous crusade to resist the flapper phenomenon in toto. According to DeBerg, that response constituted the debut of fundamentalism on the stage of American history.

Ungodly Women introduced students of fundamentalism to an uncharted mental world in which muscular Christianity, submissive wives, and reproductive families vied with a six-day creation and an end-times rapture for thematic dominance. One of its chief contributions to the literature was its demonstration of the subtle and not so subtle ways that counterrevolutionary antifeminism permeated even the supposedly pure realms of fundamentalist theology and biblical interpretation. Before DeBerg, Sandeen and Marsden had realized that fundamentalist reality did not always match the fundamentalist self-portrait. Fundamentalists said that they were earnestly contending "for the faith which was once delivered unto the saints" (Jude 3, KJV). The straight orthodoxy that fundamentalists so vigorously defended, however, turned out to be a homemade blend of undeclared theological and cultural ingredients—many dating back only as far as the nineteenth century. DeBerg discovered even more. Apparently, fundamentalists also laced their fundamentalism with large doses of reactionary gender ideology. At its core, she concluded, original fundamentalism was "an expression of widespread unease" over the demise of a once dominant "set of social conventions."[37] From her perspective, Marsden's "angry" evangelicals were vexed by more than deviant doctrine.

Ethnography: Brenda Brasher

Betty DeBerg's strategic shift from men to women, from theology to culture, and from elite fundamentalism to popular fundamentalism represented another important turning point in the methodological debate within fundamentalism studies. It also reflected the continuing expansion of the academic study of religion itself. Increasingly during the last decades of the twentieth century, as the nonconfessional discipline of religious studies became the prime location in higher education for the critical examination of religion (an "open corridor of public discourse," as Amanda Porterfield termed it[38]), the study of Protestant evangelicalism and fundamentalism looked less and less like an exercise in the study of a distinctive creed. Anthropologist Clifford Geertz's enormously influential *Islam Observed* (1968), along with his essays "Religion as a Cultural System" (1966) and "Thick Description: Toward an Interpretive Theory of Culture" (1973), had already steered many scholars away from an overly cognitive identification of religion with ideas.[39] Bruce Kuklick's critique of a "Cartesian" preoccupation with intellectual history had largely the same effect in the study of U.S. religion.[40] Ninian Smart's widely accepted phenomenological approach, set forth in *Worldviews* (1995) and a number of other publications, reminded everyone in the interdisciplinary affair of religious studies that doctrine represented only one aspect of a multifaceted reality that also included the equally or even more important dimensions of myth, ritual, experience, aesthetics, ethics, and community.[41] Following these leads, many scholars began to hunt for the heart of religion, including American fundamentalist religion, in the artifacts of material culture, the unsystematic rites of cultural practice, and the unpredictable lives of ordinary people. "Lived" religion functioned as the new center of gravity for the discipline.

For fundamentalism studies, these trends in methodology encouraged a general swing toward ethnography and what anthropologists call agents' description. Reliance upon literary, theological, and historical methods yielded to principles and procedures associated more directly with the social sciences. Humanist study of literary texts took a backseat to scientific study of human documents. Personal observation and even participant-observation, blurring the line between researcher and subject, became the privileged modes for the study of fundamentalists. Empathy emerged as its emotional signature. The most daring of the studies in this genre coupled rigorous quantitative analysis with soul-searching autobiographical reflection.

A conspicuous feature of this scholarship has been the prominence of women scholars as pacesetters in the new endeavors. Sociologist Nancy T. Ammerman, a lifelong practicing Baptist, has added three important works to the fundamentalism studies canon: *Bible Believers* (1987), based on a twelve-month stint of participant-observation in a New England fundamentalist congregation; *Baptist Battles* (1990), a frontline account of the Southern Baptist Convention's "holy war" during the 1980s; and *Southern Baptists Observed* (1993).[42] Anthropologist Ellen Rosenberg's *The Southern Baptists* (1989) also found the "fundamentalist takeover" of America's largest Protestant denomination an irresistible opportunity to study U.S. evangelicalism in the crisis of conflict and transition.[43] In *The Book of Jerry Falwell* (2000), fellow anthropologist Susan Friend Harding turned hundreds of hours of interviews and field observation into an extraordinary investigation of the "Bible-based language" of the nation's best-known Baptist fundamentalist.[44]

A discussion of Brenda Brasher's contribution to this new phase of fundamentalism studies nicely rounds out this survey of the methodological pluralism characterizing the field after 1980. A graduate of Indiana University–Purdue University Indianapolis and Christian Theological Seminary, Brasher received her PhD in religion and social ethics from the University of Southern California. Her academic career has included teaching positions at Mount Union College in Ohio and the University of Aberdeen in Scotland, as well as a Fulbright scholarship in the Ukraine. Her publications have advanced the research on topics such as gender and violence, apocalyptic movements, and the brave new world of religion in cyberspace.[45] Her editorial oversight of *The Encyclopedia of Fundamentalism* (2001), a landmark in the history of fundamentalism studies, demonstrated the promise of the "mini-industry" at the beginning of the twenty-first century. A self-described "liberal Christian" and "committed feminist," Brasher has dedicated much of her career to empathetic examination of the nonmainline Christian "other" on its own terms.[46]

Brasher's 1998 ethnographic study of female fundamentalists in the United States established her as a major interpreter of a neglected dimension of the fundamentalist phenomenon. Entitled *Godly Women,* in provocative contrast to DeBerg's *Ungodly Women,* the book sought to convey the experience of women in Protestant fundamentalism free from academic bias and oversimplification. Unlike DeBerg, Brasher addressed the second wave of American fundamentalism that gained force during the 1970s and 1980s. More important, she bypassed the printed ideas of male fundamentalists on the topic of women and concentrated exclusively on the living testimony of fundamentalist women themselves. Despite differences in method and focus, however, she agreed with DeBerg on the nontheological nature of much of the fundamentalist worldview and the "centrality of gender" for fundamentalist doctrine and discipline. According to Brasher, "At fundamentalist congregations, gender organizes material and ideal religious life—from worship to administration, from social interaction to architecture....What many fundamentalist believers overtly claim to be purely religious ideas and behaviors are significantly informed by cultural gender quarrels."[47]

Brasher's "gynocentric" and "microanalytical" research design involved her in intensive field study of women in two southern California fundamentalist congregations—one affiliated loosely with Chuck Smith's Calvary Chapel in Costa Mesa, best known for its ministry to hippies and "Jesus people" during the 1960s, and another congregation associated with a reform movement in the International Church of the Foursquare Gospel, a Pentecostal denomination founded by flamboyant evangelist Aimee Semple McPherson. Over the course of six months, Brasher participated in Bible studies, retreats, worship services, and numerous other activities sponsored by the women's ministries in the churches. She also conducted a series of two-hour interviews with selected female participants that covered issues such as conversion, religious experience, sexual identity, marriage, family life, ecclesiastical polity, recreation, and politics.

Some of Brasher's findings confirmed key elements of the scholarly consensus on fundamentalism. Her conclusion regarding the presence of a patriarchal "sacred canopy" dominating fundamentalist life and thought echoed longstanding suspicions and reaffirmed an interpretative tradition stretching back at least a decade. By the 1990s, few observers had failed to notice fundamentalism's predilection for pre-twentieth-century sexual values. Brasher's intimate encounter with a subculture replete with talk of female submission and divinely ordained male headship reemphasized academic convictions regarding fundamentalism's deeply ingrained commitment to sexual hierarchy.

Brasher also discovered in the communities ambivalent feelings toward the demands and rewards of secular modernity. Routine reference to the supernatural, defense of the nuclear family, dedication to group solidarity, and criticism of lifestyle consumerism, she said, placed female fundamentalists in direct opposition to major tenets of the American creed. At the same time, however, Brasher found few fundamentalist women who could be classed as thoroughgoing antimodernists or Victorian apologists. Many of them, she stated, demonstrated a willingness to soften standards on divorce, speak of marriage in "relatively egalitarian terms," and convert to religious purposes some of the most "seductive" symbols of modernity — symbols such as blue jeans, rock music, therapeutic language, and commercial packaging. Rather than uncritical rejection of modernity, what Brasher's fieldwork exposed was a calculating desire to "countercolonize" choice aspects of modern culture seemingly at variance with fundamentalist norms. As representatives of second-wave fundamentalism, Brasher argued, these godly women "actively attempt to reshape modernity by turning its products to their advantage."[48]

Some of Brasher's other conclusions challenged scholarly assumptions even more radically. Her analysis of a "sacred gender wall" bisecting the community underneath the "sacred canopy" raised serious questions about the place of women in a patriarchal system. Previous hypotheses about the totalizing effect of patriarchy, when they had even granted the possibility of imagining the existence of female fundamentalists, had presumed that women in fundamentalist groups functioned as shadowy, robotic figures whose very presence in the movements defied common sense. Brasher's examination of the evidence convinced

her that women constituted the majority in fundamentalist congregations just as they do in most other religious groups. She also
came to believe that women in fundamentalist groups, though
marginalized, exercise a significant degree of rational choice in
their decisions to join patriarchal churches and a considerable
amount of self-determination in governing their participation in
the churches. More important, Brasher concluded that through the
organization and maintenance of sophisticated all-female
enclaves in the congregations, fundamentalist women act as free
moral agents, creating protected zones of intellectual and ritual
leadership that simultaneously support and subvert male pastoral
authority. Though they accept patriarchy as part of a supernaturally sanctioned moral order, the godly women of second-wave
fundamentalism, according to Brasher, "bargain with patriarchy
to get what they want."[49]

Pioneering research after World War II unearthed millennial
hope at the heart of first-wave fundamentalism. More critically
nuanced approaches during the 1980s and 1990s revealed antimodern or antifeminist militancy as the driving force behind the
new aggressive movements. Brasher's thick description, along
with similarly conceived initiatives, helped to uncover the all-too-
human dimension of paradox in postresurgence fundamentalist
experience. After nearly seventy years of formal academic study,
the cultural system of American Protestant fundamentalism—
what Falwell had called "the religious phenomenon of the twentieth century"—was fast appearing both more mysterious and,
strangely, more recognizable as that century came to a close. Any
religious movement that could serve as such a "curious mixture of
empowerment and disempowerment"[50] was clearly a more complex reality than anyone had ever imagined.

4
The Fundamentalist Impulse
in Catholic Christianity

The critically acclaimed achievements of Ernest Sandeen and George Marsden secured for fundamentalism studies a respectable place in the academic study of U.S. religion. The scholars who built upon their accomplishments, including Betty DeBerg and Brenda Brasher, expanded the research base for future investigations and refined the methodological techniques that other scholars would exploit for years to come. By the beginning of the twenty-first century, academics in a wide variety of disciplines recognized the study of American Protestant fundamentalism as an intriguing, relevant, and internally diverse area of scholarly expertise.

Just as fundamentalism studies was gaining enhanced prestige in the academic community, the term *fundamentalism* took on a life of its own in public discourse. During the 1970s and 1980s, a wave of sacred rage around the globe suggested to many observers that the reappearance of Protestant fundamentalism and the rise of the New Religious Right in the United States represented only selected features of a worldwide revolt against secular modernity. The success of apocalyptic and Pentecostal Christianities in the Third World, Arab nationalism and anti-Western agitation in the Islamic world, militantly religious forms of Zionism in Judaism, and a crop of neo-traditionalist protest movements in other world religions seemed to warrant application of the category *fundamentalism* to a host of phenomena far beyond the limited realm of "angry" North American evangelicals. At first tentatively and then with greater confidence and even urgency, journalists, public officials, religious leaders, and a growing number of academics began to use *fundamentalism* as a convenient umbrella term to classify and sometimes indict late twentieth-century efforts to reclaim the modern world for God.

The following chapters will take an in-depth look at this reorientation of *fundamentalism* and the academic and interreligious debates regarding its legitimacy. This chapter begins that process by moving a few steps away from paradigmatic Protestant fundamentalism. It reviews controversial attempts to transfer the category *fundamentalism* from the economy of U.S. evangelical Protestantism to the world of modern international Catholicism. Surveying both official and popular forms of Catholic Christianity, the chapter explores scholarly attempts to reckon with the antimodernist impulse in twentieth-century Catholic thought; the emergence of countercultural Catholicisms antagonistic to Vatican II; and the growth of a Catholic underground of conspiracy theories, supernatural intrigue, and reactionary political activism.

Catholic Responses to Protestant Fundamentalism

Before we review the attempts to delineate specifically Catholic forms of fundamentalism, we should note that the advent of Protestant fundamentalism did not fail to elicit reaction from the Catholic intellectual community. After the rise of U.S. Protestant fundamentalism in the first decades of the twentieth century, Catholic scholars, journalists, and church leaders expressed interest in what they variously described as the latest form of infidelity or the most serious competitor to Catholicism in the religious marketplace. The revival of Protestant fundamentalism in the 1970s, coupled with its aggressive infiltration into Catholic strongholds such as Central and South America, sparked a series of particularly charged responses to what soon became known as "biblical Christianity."

G. K. Chesterton, leading light of the early twentieth-century Catholic Literary Revival in Britain, penned one of the first Catholic appraisals of Protestant fundamentalism. Commenting on the 1925 *Scopes* trial, he portrayed fundamentalism as truncated Christianity: "The Fundamentalists are funny enough, and the funniest thing about them is their name. For, whatever else the Fundamentalist is, he is not fundamental. He is content with the bare letter of Scripture—the translation of a translation—without venturing to ask for its original authority."[1] Identifying fundamentalism chiefly with an exaggerated *sola scriptura* and the exaltation of biblical inerrancy to creedal status, Chesterton articulated what would become a permanent theme of the Catholic critique of fundamentalism. For him, fundamentalism represented an orphan orthodoxy—Christian truth cut off from Christian church and Christian civilization.

At the same time, however, Chesterton professed grudging respect for fundamentalists. No friend of secularism or post-Darwinian science, he viewed fundamentalist-baiter H. L. Mencken and the new breed of antifundamentalists with suspicion. "It is the custom to make fun of Fundamentalism and to suggest that American religion is rather antiquated," he wrote. "But I sometimes think that American irreligion is much more antiquated than American religion, and that the sceptic can be more of a fossil than the sectarian."[2] Along with a handful of other Catholic observers, especially Americans on guard against the revival of anti-Catholic bigotry, Chesterton realized that Catholic attacks on fundamentalism could easily backfire. The church that condemned Galileo and forced the Anti-Modernist Oath on its clergy could ill afford to heap ridicule on antievolution evangelicals.[3]

Roughly half a century after *Scopes,* in the years following Vatican II, Catholic responses to Protestant fundamentalism multiplied and intensified. Apologists defended Catholic distinctives against fundamentalist assault. Postconciliar theologians, echoing an earlier generation of Protestant modernists, portrayed fundamentalism as a distorted Christianity of simplistic bibliolatry and intellectual obscurantism. Church leaders—from local bishops to Vatican officials—warned the faithful of fundamentalism's shallow spirituality and manipulative recruitment tactics. Expanding the canon of antifundamentalist literature, most of these efforts generated more heat than light. According to William Shea, an authority on Catholic-evangelical relations, Catholic responses to Protestant fundamentalism from the 1970s to the early twenty-first century showed "little sign of any serious interest in fundamentalist or evangelical theology" and betrayed "no more than a cursory knowledge of [biblical Christianity's] intellectual history or its important texts."[4]

Discovering Catholic Fundamentalisms

While some Catholics responded to the external challenge of resurgent Protestant fundamentalism, others detected signs of a fundamentalist inclination within their own ranks. A spate of articles and pamphlets appeared in the Catholic press during the 1980s, announcing the existence of surprisingly new Catholic variants of fundamentalism. Most of the essays, tracts, and editorials, written by proponents of liberal or progressive interpretations of post–Vatican II Catholicism, transposed conventional motifs from the critique of Protestant fundamentalism to a new polemic against Catholic fundamentalism. Within a decade, however, a more rigorous scholarship of Catholic fundamentalisms developed separate from the journalistic trend. By the 1990s, Catholic and non-Catholic academics, motivated in part by impressive achievements in the study of Protestant fundamentalism, had established at least what approximated a new subfield of the interdisciplinary enterprise dedicated to the critical study of fundamentalist-style movements within Catholicism. Though it

did not gain the sort of scholarly acceptance that Protestant fundamentalism studies had enjoyed since the 1980s, Catholic fundamentalism studies was nevertheless a permanent fixture in
Catholic studies by the end of the twentieth century.

The first recorded reference to a Catholic fundamentalism
actually dates back to the 1920s. A small number of lost-generation
intellectuals, estranged from traditional Christianity, tentatively
expressed a humanist appreciation for Protestant fundamentalism
and its sense of crisis in a world divorced from time-honored values. In *A Preface to Morals* (1929), Pulitzer Prize–winning editor
and political columnist Walter Lippmann suggested that fundamentalist anxiety in face of the "acids of modernity" contained within it
elements of a countervailing wisdom from which even unbelieving
moderns could benefit—especially as they contemplated the future
of civilization without the restraints of religious belief and moral
certainty. While offering guarded praise for the insights of Princeton Seminary theologian J. Gresham Machen, Lippmann also
provocatively cast an admiring eye toward what he called a "deeper
fundamentalism" with a "living authority" that Protestant fundamentalism armed with only an inerrant Bible could not rival. In the
aftermath of the Great War, Harvard literary critic Irving Babbitt
had already intimated that the Church of Rome was the lone institution that could "uphold civilized standards" in a modern wasteland
"gone wrong on first principles." A stream of postwar literary converts put that hunch into action. Lippmann's circumspect esteem
for "the oldest fundamentalism of the western world" poignantly
communicated the nostalgia and foreboding that gripped a generation "perplexed by the consequences of their own irreligion."[5]

Thirty years later, another Pulitzer Prize winner, historian
Richard Hofstadter, picked up the notion of "Catholic fundamentalism" and incorporated it into his critique of what he considered to be
the impoverishment of America's democratic culture during the
1950s. Writing for a Cold War generation gripped by its distinctively
atomic-age anxiety, Hofstadter argued that McCarthy-era Catholicism mirrored the same sort of authoritarian and self-righteous

tendencies already established within the public tradition of conservative Protestant evangelicalism. In *Anti-Intellectualism in American Life* (1962), he identified the first signs of an unusual ecumenical alignment that later observers would describe as the New Religious Right:

> Indeed, one of the most striking developments of our time has been the emergence of a kind of union, or at least a capacity for cooperation, between Protestant and Catholic fundamentalists, who share a common puritanism and a common mindless militancy on what they imagine to be political issues, which unite them in opposition to what they repetitively call Godless Communism. Many Catholics seem to have overcome the natural reluctance one might expect them to have to join hands with the very type of bigoted Protestant who scourged their ancestors. It seems a melancholy irony that a union which the common bonds of Christian fraternity could not achieve has been forged by the ecumenicism of hatred.[6]

The first Catholic critics of Catholic fundamentalism, writing in the wake of Vatican II, apparently knew nothing of Lippmann's musings on the West's "oldest fundamentalism." Nor would they have appreciated his subtle implications about the supposed genius of antimodern Catholicism. They especially would have balked at his identification of the entire Catholic tradition with a fundamentalist mentality. Their assessments of Catholic fundamentalism jibed more closely with Hofstadter's negative evaluation. For them, fundamentalism represented an alien particle in the body of genuine Catholicity, just recently renewed by the *aggiornamento* (updating) of Vatican II. Catholic fundamentalism, its first Catholic opponents asserted, was a "problem" to be solved, a "disease" to be cured—not a treasury of timeless wisdom to be tapped.[7] As Notre Dame theologian Thomas O'Meara put it, "Catholicism is the opposite of fundamentalism."[8]

The exact origins of the phrase "Catholic fundamentalism" in this sense are obscure. Benedictine monk Damien Kraus used it in a little-known article published in 1982.[9] This modest analysis was followed in the next few years by a steady flow of articles in mainstream Catholic periodicals such as *America, Commonweal,* and *New Catholic World.*[10] Catholic social scientists and scripture scholars contributed the bulk of the articles, with Old Testament specialists playing a particularly predominant role in the early phase of the conversation. Systematic theologians and church historians joined in only later. Few of the writers displayed more than minimal familiarity with the growing scholarship on Protestant fundamentalism, the natural analogue. Some focused uncritically on naïve biblical literalism as the principal characteristic of fundamentalism. Others tended to reduce the phenomenon to a psychological level, arguing mainly from anecdotal evidence. Virtually all of the writers addressed Catholic fundamentalism from a pastoral point of view.

In their attempt to come to terms with Catholic fundamentalism, the first writers in the field approached their subject in three distinctive ways. One spoke of Catholic fundamentalism as something of a perennial type, a chronic threat to authentic Catholicism lodged dangerously inside the faith. Ethical dualism, ecclesiastical exclusivism, gnostic elitism, and an ahistorical sense of tradition, it suggested, were the salient features of Catholic fundamentalism. Another approach pictured Catholic fundamentalism as peculiarly American, a byproduct of the flourishing of the Catholic charismatic movement, the triumph of the New Religious Right, and the inauguration of the U.S. culture wars. It tied Catholic fundamentalist identity to a set of factors including a heightened sense of the supernatural, a resistance to critical methods of biblical study, an attraction to evangelical styles of spirituality, an inclination toward right-wing political causes, and a zeal for apologetics and evangelization. A third approach placed Catholic fundamentalism in the more international context of an intensifying backlash against Vatican II and the allegedly restorationist agenda of Pope John Paul II and his handpicked prefect for the Congregation for the Doctrine of the Faith, Cardinal Joseph Ratzinger (now Pope Benedict XVI). According to this perspective, a return to preconciliar modes of clerical authority, a retrieval of pre–Vatican II forms of piety, a deep suspicion of democracy, and an absolute commitment to magisterial teaching on sexual ethics captured the fundamentalist mindset in contemporary Catholicism.

Gabriel Daly's "Catholicism and Modernity" (1985), perhaps the most sophisticated of all the appraisals of Catholic fundamentalism from this period, provides an excellent example of the third interpretive pattern. An Irish theologian best known for his *Transcendence and Immanence* (1980), Daly defined Catholic fundamentalism as the revival of "integralism," the dogmatic and legalistic "state of mind" that resisted the impact of post-Enlightenment thought and governed Catholic intellectual life from the papal condemnation of modernism in 1907 to Vatican II. "Authoritarian heteronomy," he argued, "can therefore rightly be seen as the Catholic form of fundamentalism, in that it treats the ecclesiastical magisterium in the same manner as the Protestant fundamentalist treats the Bible." At the same time, Daly issued one of the earliest calls for intrareligious dialogue with Catholic fundamentalists. "The ecumenical instinct to entertain and where possible to respond positively to the truth in the position of others," he wrote, "should extend also (if unilaterally) to fundamentalism. An attitude of academic contempt achieves nothing."[11]

Describing Catholic Fundamentalisms:
James Hitchcock and William Dinges

In 1989, the College Theology Society (CTS), a major professional society for U.S. Catholic theologians, devoted a significant portion of its annual meeting on "Religious Fundamentalism in the

Modern World" to a discussion of Catholic fundamentalism. The papers subsequently published in *The Struggle Over the Past* (1993) represented the American Catholic theological establishment's consensus on the issue after nearly a decade of reflection.[12] Relatively free from the "academic contempt" that Daly counseled against, they marked the transition of the study of Catholic fundamentalism from a pastoral-prescriptive approach to a more clinical-descriptive approach. An interdisciplinary conversation on "Fundamentalism as an Ecumenical Challenge" in a special issue of the journal *Concilium* (1992) edited by Hans Küng and Jürgen Moltmann, though still retaining a distinctly journalistic and theological animus against fundamentalism, reflected the same general trends on an international scale.[13]

The high-water mark of all fundamentalism studies in the twentieth century was the series of seminal articles on the topic published in connection with the Fundamentalism Project of the 1990s. More will be said about the Fundamentalism Project in the following chapter when we discuss the expansion of the scope of fundamentalism studies to embrace what many experts believe to be a global, multireligious affair. For now, we should simply note that the Fundamentalism Project, sponsored by the American Academy of Arts and Sciences, produced a virtually peerless tour de force in interdisciplinary, comparative public policy studies. Under the direction of Martin Marty and then research associate R. Scott Appleby (later history professor at Notre Dame), it published five formidable books of analysis and interpretation: *Fundamentalisms Observed* (1991), *Fundamentalisms and Society* (1993), *Fundamentalisms and the State* (1993), *Accounting for Fundamentalisms* (1994), and *Fundamentalisms Comprehended* (1995).[14] Scores of spin-offs, critiques, rejoinders, and imitations followed in the wake of the massive volumes. What unified the project was an editorial adaptation of philosopher Ludwig Wittgenstein's notion of "family resemblances" and consistent thematic reliance upon the motif of militancy. "Fighting back," the editors argued, is the hallmark of the fundamentalist experience in any religion and any culture.

During the course of the project, Marty, Appleby, and their team of collaborators viewed conservative protest movements within Catholicism as prime examples of non-Protestant Christian "fighting back" in the contemporary world. Two articles in the first volume *Fundamentalisms Observed* were quickly recognized by specialists as models of impartial inquiry into the question of Catholic fundamentalism. James Hitchcock's essay on "Catholic Activist Conservatism in the United States" portrayed a network of militantly conservative Catholics analogous to the American evangelical subculture that gained notoriety during the 1970s and 1980s. William D. Dinges's study of "Roman Catholic Traditionalism in the United States" depicted the lesser-known phenomenon of more radical forms of Catholic conservatism, within and outside official Church structures.

Both Hitchcock and Dinges pointed to the historical event of Vatican II as the single most important catalyst for antiliberal and antimodernist Catholicisms. Pope John XXIII commissioned the council to read the "signs of the times" and facilitate the Church's pastoral engagement with the modern world. Often recognized as "the decisive ecclesial event of the twentieth century,"[15] Vatican II and the forces it unleashed effected a sweeping transformation of Catholic faith and institutional life from papacy to parish. Though not officially charged with defining dogma or defending doctrine, Vatican II did produce an extraordinary set of documents that boldly reenvisioned longstanding Catholic positions on issues such as biblical interpretation, liturgical worship, religious life, Church authority, ecumenical dialogue, interfaith relations, religious freedom, and lay ministry. "Never before in the history of Catholicism," as one commentator observed, "have so many and such sudden changes been legislated and implemented which immediately touched the lives of the faithful, and never before had such a radical adjustment of viewpoint been required of them."[16] In an era of cultural revolution, political unrest, racial tension, and social upheaval, Vatican II

became a symbol of dramatic—even traumatic—change for generations of Catholics.

The worldwide Catholic response to Vatican II was wide ranging and charged with partisan emotion. Proponents hailed it as a new
Pentecost, a prelude to the modernization of basic doctrine, the
democratization of Church polity, the liberalization of canon law,
and a total overhaul of spiritual practice. Many took it to be the
emblem of the Church's long overdue appropriation of the Enlightenment legacy. Others saw it as a mandate for perpetual reformation
in Catholic Christianity. Karl Rahner, one of the new theologians
propelled into celebrity during the council, interpreted Vatican II in
near-mythic terms, calling it "a qualitative leap" in Christian history
that promised a new age of global spiritual renewal.[17]

Critics of the council contended that its boosters confused
reform with revolution. They judged some of the council's decrees
and many of the postconciliar experiments conducted in its
"spirit" to be unwarranted accommodations to the worst aspects of
modernity. They derided new departures in liturgy and theology as
signs of a foolish rejection of classical Christianity's cultural treasure. Opponents of liturgical change in particular shuddered at
what they considered a reckless iconoclasm bordering on vandal-
ism. Some linked a loss of reverence and majesty in worship to an
erosion of transcendence in worldview and a lowering of standards in morality. Some saw an entire cosmology at stake.[18]

Taking Protestant fundamentalism's reactive character as
axiomatic, Hitchcock and Dinges identified postconciliar Catholic
conservative and traditionalist movements as fundamentalist inso-
far as they depend upon resistance or opposition for their raison
d'être. In the case of the allegedly moderate fundamentalism of
Catholic activist conservatism, resistance is aimed at perceived
abuses of and deviance from the limited reform agenda authorized
by Vatican II. The more extreme Catholic traditionalism, arguably a
more viable candidate for a Catholic fundamentalism, disputes the
very legitimacy of the council and the popes who sanctioned it. As
both types of putative Catholic fundamentalism see it, the dominant

culture of the industrialized West represents a hostile environment for revealed religion.

When Hitchcock spoke of a sense of crisis in Church and culture motivating conservative Catholic activists, he added insider's perspective to objective analysis. At the time of his participation in the Fundamentalist Project, he was an acknowledged leader of the conservative Catholic community in America. Saint Louis University historian, legal scholar, and a founder of the intentionally orthodox Fellowship of Catholic Scholars, Hitchcock has devoted much of his career to causes associated with the values of traditional Catholicism. A number of his works, including *The Decline and Fall of Radical Catholicism* (1971), *The Recovery of the Sacred* (1974), and *Catholicism and Modernity: Confrontation or Capitulation?* (1979), have become minor classics in the canon of conservative Catholicism.[19]

In his Fundamentalism Project article, Hitchcock offered a sympathetic yet critical portrait of "a new and unprecedented brand of American Catholic activism." His research uncovered an institutionally rich and socially engaged Catholic community, whose members see themselves as doubly alienated from a decadent mainstream culture and a polarized Church permeated by permissiveness and dissent. He isolated a couple of organizations for close examination: (1) the lay group Catholics United for the Faith (CUF), founded by former stock broker H. Lyman Stebbins in 1968, the year of contentious debate over *Humane vitae* (Pope Paul VI's condemnation of artificial contraception); and (2) Opus Dei, the international fellowship founded in 1928 by Monsignor Josemaria Escriva (canonized by John Paul II in 2002)—perhaps best known for its negative pop culture portrait in Dan Brown's controversial novel *The Da Vinci Code* (2003). What distinguishes conservative Catholic activists in these and other groups from their coreligionists, according to Hitchcock, is their profession of complete fidelity to magisterial teaching, including the Church's ban on birth control, and a "strict constructionist" approach to the documents of Vatican II, stressing continuity with preconciliar tradition and the original intent of the council fathers. What qualifies them at least tentatively as fundamentalists, he said, is a cluster of attributes typically found among their Protestant counterparts: ambivalence toward modernity, attraction to culturally "scandalous" aspects of faith, an inclination toward innovative adaptations of tradition, and a willingness to collaborate with cobelligerents on front-line moral issues. Perhaps the most intriguing dimension of the conservative Catholic ethos, Hitchcock suggested, is the tension between its affirmation of Church authority and its propensity toward anticlericalism, a trait normally associated with the Church's left wing. From his perspective, a deep sense of betrayal at the hands of their own clergy places the "loyal insiders" of Catholic activist conservatism at odds with the very Church they aspire to defend.[20]

A similar, albeit greatly intensified, sense of betrayal lies at the heart of what Dinges called Roman Catholic traditionalism. Since he wrote on the topic for an American studies PhD at the University of Kansas, right-wing dissent among American Catholics has been the centerpiece of his research agenda. From his position on the religious studies faculty at the Catholic University of America and as associate editor for *U.S. Catholic Historian,* Dinges has played a key role in guiding the scholarly conversation on the spirituality of disaffected Catholics, especially young adult Catholics.[21] A working paper for Notre Dame's Cushwa Center for the Study of American Catholicism, an entry on "Fundamentalism" for *The New Dictionary of Theology* (1987), and other publications helped to lay the groundwork for his Fundamentalism Project contribution. In *Fundamentalisms Observed,* he maintained that while several Catholic organizations and schools of thought may exhibit elements of a generically fundamentalist "orientation," only the radicals of post–Vatican II traditionalism have constructed a genuinely Catholic fundamentalist "movement."[22]

Dinges's article provided the first diachronic survey of Catholic traditionalism. It traced the narrative of discontent's development into deliberate dissent and documented the appearance of alternatives to postconciliar Catholicism on the Vatican's right flank. At the time that he wrote, the history of the movement stretched from the 1965 publication of U.S. "rebel priest" Gommar De Pauw's "Catholic Traditionalist Manifesto" to the years just after the 1991 death of excommunicated French Archbishop Marcel Lefebvre, the international symbol of anticonciliar recalcitrance.

By all accounts, Lefebvre and his organization set the agenda for reactionary Catholicism during its formative period. Lefebvre, who began his career as a missionary in Africa among the Holy Ghost Fathers, went on record against Vatican II during the council itself. He found the Declaration on Religious Liberty *(Dignitatis humanae)* and the Pastoral Constitution on the Church in the Modern World *(Gaudium et spes)* especially unacceptable. After 1970, his priestly fraternity, the Society of St. Pius X (named after the pope who condemned modernism in 1907), became the nerve center of opposition to what he considered "neo-modernist" Rome. In a series of addresses and writings, including *I Accuse the Council!* (1976) and *Open Letter to Confused Catholics* (1985), he articulated his critique of the liturgical, doctrinal, and moral dimensions of postconciliar Catholicism, calling the council "the French Revolution of the Church."[23] John Paul II's policy of detente toward right-wing dissidents sparked a series of unsuccessful negotiations with the movement. When Lefebvre defied Vatican authority and independently consecrated four bishops in 1988, he pushed his movement into formal schism. Followers who defected to the papally approved Society of St. Peter were allowed to retain their antimodernist charism on condition of obedience to Rome. In a Church body already afflicted by numerous thorns on its left side, Lefebvre continued to be the most notorious irritant on the Church's right until his death.[24] Dinges described Lefebvre's legacy of unrepentant traditionalism as the most important force in the movement's uncertain future.

Dinges' article also addressed traditionalism synchronically. He arranged his analysis around a number of basic themes, including liturgy, ideology, politics, and ecclesiology. Liturgically, he said, traditionalists are set apart by their fervent disapproval or wholesale rejection of Paul VI's vernacular *Novus Ordo* Mass (1969) and their unyielding devotion to the Latin Tridentine liturgy, the rite that, with occasional modifications, had defined Catholic worship in the West from the Council of Trent to Vatican II. Dinges characterized traditionalism's theological stance as exclusive allegiance to an unchanging worldview of objective truth and supernatural reality, a full paradigm shift away from the basic assumptions of post-Enlightenment thought. He described its political vision as a recapitulation of premodern Christendom. Lefebvre's sympathy for the ancien régime gave the movement a distinctly Old World flavor.

On the issue of the Church, however, Dinges found Catholic traditionalists anything but traditional. From the underground church of unapproved Latin Masses to so-called *sedevacantist* separatists who claim that the chair of St. Peter has been vacant since the papacy of Pius XII, Catholic traditionalists have shown a decided proclivity for institutional improvisation. Some have abandoned what pioneer sociologist of religion Ernst Troeltsch called the classic civilization-centered "church" type in favor of Catholic equivalents of the countercultural "sect" type, an ecclesiological stance usually indicative of the Protestant free church tradition. This quality alone, Dinges argued, aligns Catholic traditionalists with a fundamentalist impulse provocatively similar to the one that transformed twentieth-century Protestantism. While Hitchcock hedged on full identification of conservative activists with a pan-Christian fundamentalist mindset, Dinges attempted to make a case for *Catholic fundamentalism* as a descriptive formula capable of apprehending a new reality in contemporary Catholic life.

Mapping the Catholic Right:
Mary Jo Weaver and R. Scott Appleby

The Fundamentalism Project raised awareness of fundamentalism studies in all quarters of the academy and among educated lay readers in many parts of the world. It convinced many in government and the media that the multifaceted phenomenon of fundamentalism was worthy of serious and unbiased scrutiny. Likewise, the MacArthur Foundation's role in underwriting the project persuaded other private funding agencies that fundamentalism studies was a promising new area for financial investment and institutional support.

In Catholic circles, the Fundamentalism Project gave impetus to further exploration of the question of Catholic fundamentalisms. It brought fresh insights and new precision to the ongoing and sometimes heated conversation. The highly publicized discussion of fundamentalism also provoked responses from right-of-center Catholics who, despite disavowals of "academic contempt," still perceived the labeling process as indiscriminate and prejudicial. Criticism from the right tended to view the implied conservative/liberal dichotomy as an overpoliticization of basically spiritual matters.[25]

An excellent example of the continuing interest in Catholic fundamentalisms was a volume prepared by another team of scholars assembled just after the Fundamentalism Project began to gain momentum. The purpose of this mapping project, as the directors described it, was to chart the landscape of the postconciliar American conservative Catholic experience—fundamentalist and otherwise. Funded by a grant from the Lilly Endowment, the project produced a set of essays that scanned the varieties of U.S. conservative Catholicism from both insider and outsider perspectives. After the release of *Being Right: Conservative Catholics in America* (1995), a similarly collaborative process led to a companion volume called *What's Left? Liberal American*

Catholics (1999), a conceptual map of the other side of U.S. Catholic culture.[26]

The principal cartographers who designed the survey of America's Catholic right brought to their task expertise in U.S. religious history and a desire to execute "a serious and respectful study of Catholics who seem to have been overlooked by mainstream scholars of religion."[27] Mary Jo Weaver, professor emerita of religious studies and women's studies at Indiana University, began her career as a specialist in the history of European Catholic modernism. Her books *New Catholic Women* (1986), *Springs of Water in a Dry Land* (1993), and *Cloister and Community* (2002) have confirmed her reputation as a major authority on and advocate for feminism in contemporary Catholic Christianity.[28] Her article on "The Fundamentalist Challenge" in the 1989 CTS annual volume and her entry on "Catholic Fundamentalism" in Brenda Brasher's *Encyclopedia of Fundamentalism* demonstrated her interpretive grasp of Christianities other than her own. Her colleague, R. Scott Appleby, protégé of Martin Marty and co-director of the Fundamentalism Project, also began his career writing on Catholic modernism—in his case, the lesser-known American kind. He, too, participated in the 1989 CTS discussion of fundamentalism. After joining the history department at the University of Notre Dame, he directed the Cushwa Center for the Study of American Catholicism and then the Joan B. Kroc Institute for International Peace Studies. Numerous publications, such as *The Ambivalence of the Sacred* (2000), have established him as a leading authority on global religious conflict and reconciliation.[29]

Major figures in the U.S. Catholic community contributed to *Being Right,* including two veterans of the Fundamentalism Project. Hitchcock wrote on the history and mission of the Fellowship of Catholic Scholars, calling its members a "cognitive minority" in both American Catholic higher education and the country's broader intellectual scene.[30] Dinges updated his research on Catholic traditionalism, tracking the development of key and sometimes obscure organizations such as the Catholic Traditionalist

Movement, the Orthodox Roman Catholic Movement, the Tridentine Latin Rite Church, the Tridentine Rite Conference, the Society of Traditional Roman Catholics, as well as the better known Society of St. Pius X, Society of St. Peter, and the Society of St. Pius V, a separatist spin-off from Lefebvre's group.

Chapters from prominent insiders included a survey of the work of CUF by its vice president James Sullivan and a review of the philosophy and accomplishments of the antifeminist Women for Faith and Family by its founder Helen Hull Hitchcock. An essay on "neoconservative" Catholics by theologian/commentator George Weigel, now well known for his bestselling biography of John Paul II, exposed the inadequacy of a two-party model when applied uncritically to U.S. Catholic life. What Weigel called the "neoconservative difference" claims to reconcile ecumenical Christian orthodoxy with the political pragmatism and free market economic theory of the "American experiment." His call for a "*public* church" not a "*partisan* church" would arguably strike many fellow conservative Catholics as dangerously close to liberal Catholicism's alleged compromise with mainstream American culture.[31]

The book's outsider analyses concentrated on other dimensions of America's conservative Catholic subculture. Weaver's study of "self-consciously countercultural" colleges—Thomas Aquinas (California), Magdalen (New Hampshire), Christendom (Virginia), and Thomas More (New Hampshire)—underscored the central role of ideas in conservative Catholics' quarrel with religious modernism and secular modernity. According to her findings, these lay-founded and lay-run schools, marginal to both the state-supported and Catholic university systems, see themselves as responding to an "intellectual identity crisis among Catholics" and offering the only authentic implementation of *Ex corde ecclesiae* (1990), John Paul II's directives on Catholic higher education.[32]

Sandra Zimdars-Swartz, an authority on modern devotion to the Virgin Mary, explored a more experiential dimension of conservative Catholicism. Her examination of the unexpected postconciliar revival of Marian piety emphasized the important place of supernaturalism in the subculture's worldview. For some conservative Catholics, she said, the reported apparitions of the Virgin Mary in Medjugorje, Yugoslavia, during the 1980s and the careers of American visionaries Nancy Fowler and Estela Ruiz reveal the signs of the times far more powerfully than official episcopal synods or Vatican documents.

Michael Cuneo, whose work is discussed more fully in the following section, shed light on still another dimension of conservative Catholicism: ethics and social activism. He traced the radicalization of a segment of the conservative Catholic community to the watershed year 1973, when in *Roe v. Wade* the U.S. Supreme Court legalized abortion on demand in America. His description of the militant subgroup's appropriation of civil disobedience methods and ecumenical strategies documented a remarkable reorientation in U.S. religion. His definition of antiabortion protest as a "ritual of cultural defiance" represented a breakthrough for interpretations of pro-life agitation otherwise baffled by some activists' apparent apathy toward practical results.[33]

Generally both the insiders and the outsiders in *Being Right* exhibited either reluctance or refusal to invoke *fundamentalism* as a controlling concept. Appleby had staked his career on the term. He was already on record defending the term as a comparative category for "oppositional movements" issuing from embattled religious enclaves.[34] Few of the other authors, however, explicitly endorsed the term's application to things Catholic. Some of the insiders expressed concern over the use of any adjective to modify *Catholic*. If Catholic identity hinges on assent to Church teaching and conformity to Church law, they insisted, then distinctions such as left-wing, right-wing, liberal, conservative, fundamentalist—even orthodox—are ultimately at odds with the way that the Catholic tradition defines itself.

Weaver cautiously entertained *fundamentalism* as a conceptual catalyst for critical reflection but suspected that the term was freighted too heavily with assumptions foreign to the Catholic experience to be imported duty-free into the field of Catholic studies. In her CTS paper she had spoken loosely of Protestant fundamentalism's Catholic "cousin." Later in Brasher's *Encyclopedia of Fundamentalism,* she employed the term more along the lines of Appleby's comparative approach. Still, she concluded, the concept of Catholic fundamentalism "has to admit some ambiguity of definition."[35]

Being Right captured the mood of the Catholic academic community at the end of the twentieth century. Scholars of Catholicism, particularly specialists in North American Catholicism, were intensely interested in discovering creative and effective ways to study a diverse Catholic community fractured by revolutionary and counterrevolutionary forces. They experienced division in their own ranks, however, when it came to fundamentalism.

Exploring the Catholic Underground: Michael W. Cuneo

The study of and debate over Catholic fundamentalism developed over a track comparable to the course set by Protestant fundamentalism scholarship. Modernist polemic was followed by impartial analysis, which itself was succeeded by an ethnographic turn. In the case of Catholic fundamentalism studies, however, all of this occurred over a much shorter span of time.

The empirical nature of the ethnographic turn allowed Catholic fundamentalism studies to eliminate much of the speculative quality that had hampered its initial phase. It also allowed researchers in the field to gain valuable firsthand contact with fundamentalism as a living entity. Some of the architects of the modern study of Protestant fundamentalism, such as Sandeen and Marsden, had had the advantage of childhood associations with the fundamentalist community that arguably enriched their research in immeasurable ways. For them, fundamentalism was a familiar force in both their past and their present. By contrast, most scholars of Catholic fundamentalism, even those affiliated with the Church, were not able to approach their subject with the same mix of imagination, intuition, and critical insight. For them, fundamentalism was only a present reality—and a new one at that. Saddled with the challenge of fundamentalisms distant from their personal experience, not to mention a problematic organizing principle alien to Catholic life itself, scholars of Catholic fundamentalism at the end of the twentieth century required a stronger, more reliable empirical base for their academic endeavors. This state of affairs made the ethnographic turn all that more important.

The insider reports in *Fundamentalisms Observed* and *Being Right* provided some much-needed empirical density. Weaver's essay on the conservative subculture's alternative colleges demonstrated the potential of field observation for Catholic fundamentalism studies. Since the mid-1990s, many scholars have recognized Michael Cuneo's work, exploring the near and far right of North American Catholicism, as a model of cutting-edge ethnographic fieldwork with direct bearing on the question of Catholic fundamentalisms.

A sociologist at Fordham University, Cuneo has spent most of his career studying what many people might dismiss as the "lunatic fringe" of contemporary society: exorcists, visionaries, "sidewalk counselors," conspiracy theorists, religious survivalists, death row converts, and at least one self-proclaimed pope on the run from the law. His attraction to the eccentric, his penchant for personal observation, and his lively first-person style have earned him a reputation as something of a social science thrill-seeker. His *Catholics Against the Church* (1989), a case study of antiabortion protest in Toronto, represented one of the first serious efforts to comprehend the single-issue Catholicism of radical pro-life activism and its open contempt for the institutional Church. In *American Exorcism* (2001), he combined eyewitness accounts and clinical analysis to produce one of the few academic treatments of demonic possession and its worldview. With *Almost Midnight* (2004), he entered the genre of true-crime

narrative, telling the remarkable tale of a convicted Ozarks mur-
derer who attracted the attention of John Paul II.[36]

The Smoke of Satan (1997) has been Cuneo's most important contribution to Catholic fundamentalism studies. He
intended it to be a "guided tour of the [right-wing] Catholic
underground."[37] Based on extensive travel and personal interviews, the book became the Catholic answer to the fieldwork of
Ammerman, Harding, and Brasher—and implicitly the test of all
provisional maps of contemporary Catholicism's terra incognita.
It took its provocative title from a comment attributed to Paul VI
during the bleak years of his papacy when the Church of Vatican
II reaped the whirlwind of confusion, dissent, and disillusionment
on a global scale. In counterpoint to John XXIII's sunny vision of
a well-ventilated Church, Paul allegedly observed that "Satan's
smoke has made its way into the temple of God through some
crack" (June 29, 1972). Cuneo's informants, although they disagreed on a host of issues, including even the authenticity of
Paul's papacy, would not have disagreed substantially with that
sentiment. They were of one mind when it came to the conviction
that a severe crisis was afflicting the Catholic Church.

Cuneo's guides through the Catholic underworld represented a broad sampling of major and minor figures in the conservative and traditionalist Catholic communities of the United
States and Canada (the neo-conservative circle of George Weigel,
Richard John Neuhaus, and Michael Novak being the significant
exception). The individuals ranged from the well-known "guerrilla journalist" E. Michael Jones and *Wanderer* editor Alphonse
Matt, Jr., to the more obscure Nicholas Gruner, a circuit-riding
priest in the Marian apparition network, and Mark Pivarunas,
a bishop in the lineage of renegade Vietnamese archbishop
Ngo-Dinh-Thuc. Important stops on Cuneo's tour included the St.
Louis living room of James and Helen Hitchcock (center-right), a
hippie-style commune in Kentucky opposed to the "contraceptive
mentality" (right-of-center), a breakaway Society of St. Pius V
chapel in Oyster Bay, Long Island (to the right of Lefebvre's

group), Mount St. Michael's *sedevacantist* community in Spokane, Washington (farther to the right), and the isolationist Apostles of Infinite Love in St. Jovite, Quebec (so far to the right that its practices of shared possessions, female ordination, and vernacular liturgy tilt it toward the left).[38]

To come to terms with the wide variety of experiences and concerns on the Catholic right, Cuneo divided his subjects into four rough categories. First, there were the "displaced intellectuals" of moderately mainstream conservatism—Hitchcock's "loyal insiders" who, as Cuneo put it, "find themselves in the peculiar position of claiming support for a council they secretly wish had never taken place." Next Cuneo singled out the pro-life activists whose sometimes violent extremism, he claimed, indicates a hunger for a sort of "religious virtuosity" that they cannot find in the casual Catholicism of suburban America. A third category Cuneo reserved for the ecclesiastical and liturgical separatists who operate in what he dubbed a "complex shadowlands of steamy prophecy, exotic conspiracy, and sectarian intrigue." Here he found not only fertile theories of Jewish, Masonic, and communist plots for world conquest, but also a full spectrum of grassroots speculation about kidnapped popes, imposter popes, and divinely ordained popes hiding in North America. Finally, Cuneo created a fourth category for the subculture's Marian enthusiasts—mystically inclined Catholics, like the followers of the late "Bayside seer" Veronica Lueken, whose beliefs in apocalyptic prophecy, divine secrets, supernatural scents, and miraculous photographs have thrust them into varying degrees of "cognitive dissonance" with the dominant culture of secular America.[39]

Cuneo's conclusions, echoing Hitchcock and Dinges, made important distinctions between the ordinary discontent of Catholic conservatives committed to a "reform of the reform" and the extraordinary disaffection of traditionalists and supernaturalists who frame their quarrel with postconciliar Catholicism in radical and mythic terms. The conservatives' emphasis on lay initiative, their openness to female leadership, and their non-negotiable loyalty to *Humane vitae* set them apart, he said, from the priest-centered and highly patriarchal traditionalist movements, which for one reason or another do not see birth control as a cardinal theological issue.

What Cuneo found most striking about the traditionalist and apocalyptic groups was the curiously American and "Protestant" tenor of their spirituality. Historians have long identified separatism and sectarianism as signature themes of the American religious experience. Evidences of the free church tradition's unmitigated triumph in the New World—soul-liberty and the image of the earnest individual seeker—have become for many Americans synonymous with religion itself. According to Cuneo, these modes of pragmatic experiment and prophetic critique are deeply ingrained in all dimensions of the far right Catholic phenomenon. In their opposition to what they perceive to be Vatican II's canonization of Protestant norms and their quest to out-Catholic the pope, Cuneo argued, traditionalists unwittingly imitate the very thing they most fervently seek to avoid. Likewise, he said, the new Marianists, despite their intense devotion to the Virgin of La Salette, Fatima, and Medjugorje, seem to have much more in common with Protestant premillennialists than with pre-modern Catholics. Even the inaugural encyclical of one of traditionalism's self-declared popes (Gregory XVII of the Infinite Love community)—with its condemnation of smoking, drinking, and mixed swimming and its prophecy of Rome's capitulation to Antichrist—could easily be mistaken for a page torn from the book of American revivalism. "With their perfectionist aspirations, their cultural exclusivity, and their spiritual elitism," Cuneo wrote, "[Catholic] separatists are participants in an American tradition of religious utopianism that extends at least as far back as Plymouth Rock."[40]

French philosopher Jacques Maritain, himself no fan of Vatican II's *aggiornamento,* once observed that "Americans seem to be in their own land as pilgrims, prodded by a dream."[41] Cuneo used the same sort of language to summarize what he considered to be the very American, very Protestant "mood" of Catholic traditionalists and supernaturalists. He described their underground empire, densely crowded with upstart institutions and charismatic leaders, as the dark Catholic twin of the above-ground landscape of American evangelical and Pentecostal denominationalism. He also interpreted their unfettered quest for sacred purity as the unmistakable mark of participation in the American tradition of perpetual pilgrimage, if not fugitive spirituality. From Cuneo's vantage point, the drive of the traditionalists, activists, and supernaturalists to rescue Catholic substance from a self-destructing Roman Church ironically has transformed them into nothing less than modernity's latest variation of Protestant principle.

But are they fundamentalists? In *Catholics Against the Church,* Cuneo directly addressed the problem of "naming the subculture." He agreed with skeptics who warned that "facile comparisons" between conservative Catholics and fundamentalists of other traditions would distort the available evidence and harness technical language to personal prejudice. At the same time, he maintained that objective analysis of the data could not deny "several suggestive points of comparison" obtaining between radical Catholic pro-life activism and Protestant fundamentalism: "Both represent protests against modernizing trends within the wider culture and within their parent churches, both espouse an ideology of cultural decline, both attempt a puritan retrieval of core elements of their respective traditions, and both have cemented their distinctive identities through political activism."[42]

In *The Smoke of Satan,* Cuneo revisited these issues, expanding the scope of the discussion to include all manifestations of the Catholic right. He specifically indicted scholars who dismiss Catholic fundamentalism as a "conceptual lost cause" for indulging in unproductive "definitional dogmatism." At the very least, he said, "fundamentalism" functions as a profitable "heuristic concept" for Catholic studies, an investigative lens that can bring clarity and depth to a researcher's analytic vision—especially on a new frontier of study. As far as he was concerned, it was a useful instrument for analysis and classification, proven in the field, with few satisfactory alternatives.[43]

As the twenty-first century got underway, Cuneo's colleagues in the study of American Catholicism still had mixed feelings about *Catholic fundamentalism* as a formal category. Specialists in other areas of Catholic life and thought continued to express reservations as well. Those who agreed with him argued that the strange new world of alternative Catholicisms demanded a new working vocabulary. When Catholics, just as "angry" as Marsden's militant evangelicals, challenge not only modern decadence and disbelief but also historic Vatican legitimacy, they said, the old theological lexicon needs an *aggiornamento* of its own. Critics smelled smoke in the temple, too, but insisted that talk about Catholic fundamentalisms was simply playing with fire.

Meanwhile, white smoke announced the election of Benedict XVI in 2005, to the delight of conservative Catholics around the globe. The tone for his papacy was set by his homily at the beginning of the conclave following John Paul's funeral. Portraying contemporary Christianity as endangered by many winds of doctrine (from Marxism and atheism to syncretism and a new "dictatorship of relativism"), he also attempted to distinguish genuine Christian faith from fundamentalism. "Today," he said, "having a clear faith based on the Creed of the Church is often labeled as fundamentalism."[44] The unusual reference, witnessed by the entire world thanks to nonstop media coverage, not only reinforced the place of Curtis Lee Laws's American neologism in public papal discourse but virtually guaranteed continuing debate on the question of Catholic fundamentalism.

5
Comparative Fundamentalism Studies: Islam

Few of the scholars who adopted *fundamentalism* as a technical term for antimodern modes of Catholic identity after Vatican II failed to notice the built-in international character of the phenomenon. A defiant French archbishop, a renegade Vietnamese bishop, a modern-day saint in Spain, a Marian pilgrimage site in the Balkans, and a wildcat "pope" or two in Canada meant that Catholic fundamentalism—whatever its precise definition—could never be reduced to one theater of the U.S. culture war. After the 1970s, scholars of Protestant fundamentalism recognized that, though admittedly made in the U.S.A., it too possessed an intriguing multinational quality.

One collaborative study from the 1990s, examining the full sweep of U.S.-based missionary outreach and satellite TV ministries around the planet, declared Protestant fundamentalism and Pentecostalism to be among America's most successful export industries. Receptive Third World audiences, attracted to the "health and wealth" message of American televangelists, engaged by the experiential temper of their supernaturalist spirituality, and, in some cases, lured by the financial promises of a U.S. foreign policy sanctioned by the Religious Right, transformed the "American gospel" into a "transnational religious culture." American superstars such as Billy Graham, Oral Roberts, Pat Robertson, Jimmy Swaggart, and Kenneth Copeland set the pattern for David Yonggi Cho in South Korea, pastor of Seoul's Yoido Full Gospel Church, the world's largest congregation, and Reinhard Bonnke in sub-Sahara Africa, the "world's most successful tent evangelist." Economic globalization and the spread of entrepreneurial born-again Christianity proceeded hand in hand.[1] In the last years of the twentieth century, Christian fundamentalisms, almost by definition the religions of self-conscious remnants, acquired the cachet of truly universal movements.

While academics and religious leaders measured the extended proportions of Christian fundamentalisms around the world, unanticipated references to new, non-Christian fundamentalisms were transfiguring the vocabularies and worldviews of Western media moguls and political pundits. Virtually overnight, English-language press coverage of the 1979 Islamic Revolution in Iran established fundamentalism as a portable interpretive category. Applicable, in theory at least, to an unlimited set of contexts outside the scope of neo-traditionalist Christianities, *fundamentalism* swiftly became one of the most controversial American English loan words in modern history. George Marsden's attention to "generic" fundamentalism in *Fundamentalism and American Culture* indicated the degree to which the issue had begun to impinge upon the study of classical Protestant fundamentalism by 1980.[2] Talk of Islamic fundamentalism even preceded and, to a degree, precipitated the quest for Catholic fundamentalisms. Soon it became commonplace to speak of fundamentalism as a type of religious orientation with no necessary connection to North American culture or defensive Christian faith.

This chapter and the following one travel far beyond the world of Christian—Protestant and Catholic—fundamentalisms. They guide the reader through the ever-expanding critical literature on the varieties of global fundamentalist experience, examining the works of pioneering researchers who have viewed fundamentalism as a mythic vision, ideology, or worldview capable of finding a niche in nearly any religious tradition. According to these scholars, critical investigation into phenomena such as Jewish separatism, Zionist radicalism, Hindu nationalism, Sikh communalism, Buddhist sectarianism, and the multinational Islamic resurgence reveals global patterns of retrenchment and resentment that demand common analysis and comparative interpretation.

Karl Jasper's famous notion of an "axial age" uniting Gautama, Confucius, Zoroaster, Pythagoras, Socrates, and Isaiah into a five- to six-century span of altered consciousness allowed comparative religion scholars of the 1950s and 1960s to speculate creatively about transcendent bonds linking the "great souls" of ancient civilizations.[3] By the late 1970s, the concept of fundamentalism had begun to function as a similarly synthetic interpretive scheme for a new generation of culture watchers concerned about an axis of sacred rebellion emerging in modern history. Their various attempts to document and explain antimodernist movements in world religions eventually led to a comprehensive redefinition of fundamentalism as a globally relevant descriptive category.

Redefining Fundamentalism

The catalyst for redefinition was the Islamic Revolution in Iran. Inspired by exiled Shi'ite theologian Ayatollah Ruhollah Mussaui Khomeini, left-leaning intellectuals, middle-class merchants, urban workers, university students, and conservative religious jurists joined forces in the 1970s to topple what was perceived to be the repressive and pro-Western monarchy of Shah Muhammad Reza Pahlavi. What they achieved, after Khomeini's triumphant return to Iran in 1979, was the creation of a bold new entity in Cold War history—a constitutional theocratic republic, endowed with natural oil resources and strategic geographical location, opposed to both secular capitalism and atheistic communism, and fiercely committed to the full implementation of Muslim law as interpreted by religious elites.

In the early months of the revolution, Western media fixated on images of mass demonstrations in the streets of Iranian cities—especially self-flagellating throngs of black-garbed men chanting anti-American slogans and women in full *chador* toting automatic weapons. Then came the seizure of the U.S. embassy in Tehran by militant students and the ensuing 444-day hostage crisis that gripped the American psyche and crippled Jimmy Carter's bid for reelection. Subsequent bombings of the U.S. embassy and a Marine installation in Lebanon, followed by a spate of violent airline highjackings, convinced the Reagan administration in the early 1980s that revolutionary Iran had embarked on a mission of state-sponsored terrorism. Coinciding with the political ascent of the New Religious Right in the United States, these events galvanized American awareness of the formidable and unpredictable power of muscular antimodern religion at home and abroad. Just as Jerry Falwell personified America's new activist Protestant fundamentalism, Iran's Khomeini rapidly became the international face of virulent non-Christian fundamentalism.

The transfer of *fundamentalism* from a limited Christian to an open-ended interreligious idiom happened quickly. Journalists were in the vanguard, but government officials, historians, social scientists, psychologists, and theologians were not far behind. By the mid-1980s, an augmented sense of *fundamentalism* permeated all levels of public and academic discourse—from network news and State Department briefings to pulpit rhetoric and peer-reviewed monographs. A flood of critiques and commentaries delivered the discussion about global fundamentalism to millions of people unacquainted with the critical literature on Protestant fundamentalism. Videos, cable television, talk radio, and eventually the Internet pulled many more individuals into the conversation over the next few years. Soon everyone was saying something about fundamentalism.

The problem that stalked the new approach to the term was the need for a rigorous definition that would satisfy multiple audiences (including so-called fundamentalists themselves) and meet journalistic and academic standards at the same time. In *Islam Observed* (1968), Clifford Geertz had noticed that the comparative study of religion was plagued by the embarrassing "elusiveness of its subject matter."[4] Now the fledgling comparative study of fundamentalisms was confronting its own set of potentially embarrassing questions. If mega-church pastors engaged in a "hostile takeover" of the Southern Baptist Convention and radical mullahs fomenting revolution in the Middle East were all fundamentalists, then what exactly did *fundamentalism* mean? Why should offended Christians protesting *The Last Temptation of Christ* outside America's suburban cinemas and outraged Muslims protesting Salman Rushdie's *The Satanic Verses* in the streets of New Delhi be lumped under the same terminological umbrella? What evidence could be marshaled to demonstrate that fundamentalism constituted a multireligious, global reality?

Journalists tackled these questions with varying levels of competence and comprehension. Syndicated columnists gave Western readers a crash course on the long view of historical perspective. Cub reporters scrambled to sort out fundamentalist from Pentecostal, Sunna from Shi'a. Some writers, integrating *fundamentalism* into their work for the first time, used the term crudely and cavalierly, with only the most improvisational of definitions.

Foreign correspondent Robin Wright's *Sacred Rage: The Wrath of Militant Islam* (1985) provides an example of how the failure to digest fully the concept of fundamentalism marred an otherwise responsible treatment of resurgent Islam. Despite her intent to shed light on state-sponsored terrorism and exonerate ordinary Muslims, Wright capitalized on the evocative quality of the undefined word *fundamentalist*—as if the term itself possessed occult power to communicate all that needed to be said about radical Islam. Like a number of other writers, she invoked the term simply to clinch her main argument: "The roots of the [Islamic terrorist] trend date back thirteen centuries, and have more to do with the fanatic adherents of religious groups than with the leadership of a single country. They are fundamentalists."[5]

Similar developments obtained in the halls of government. Foreign policy statements during and after the Iranian Revolution were often hampered by uncritical reductionism. Diplomats, White House advisors, and intelligence authorities viewed fundamentalism as thinly veiled Machiavellian ambition or simply pathological hatred masquerading as traditional faith. Echoing what had been said of emergent Protestant fundamentalism decades earlier, one former State Department official spoke of late twentieth-century Islamic fundamentalism as "essentially a sociopolitical protest movement sugarcoated with religious pieties." According to R. Scott Appleby, a rash of "spectacular blunders" in America's foreign policy establishment during the 1970s and 1980s sprang from such mistaken assumptions.[6]

In the academy, comparative studies of fundamentalisms — Christian, Islamic, and otherwise — began to appear in the aftermath of the Iranian Revolution. As Duke University historian of religion Bruce Lawrence confessed in *Defenders of God: The Fundamentalist Revolt Against the Modern Age* (1989), such projects would never have been contemplated without the "shock" of the revolution in Iran.[7] Many of the best works on the topic were released around or in the years just after the 1989 death of Khomeini. Lionel Caplan, seasoned anthropologist at London's School of Oriental and African Studies, set a high standard for the new subfield with his edited volume *Studies in Religious Fundamentalism* (1987). Along with Bruce Lawrence's book, a handful of the most influential works that followed included sociologist Martin Riesebrodt's *Fundamentalismus als patriarchalische Protestbewegung* (1990, translated into English in 1993), political scientist Gilles Kepel's *La Revanche de Dieu* (1991, translated in 1994), and *Fundamentalism, Mythos, and World Religions* (1993) by historian of religion Niels Nielsen.[8] From the beginning, the enterprise was international and interdisciplinary.

The prime challenge facing such projects was to strike the right balance between analysis of empirical data from the field and critical reflection on the theoretical construct of fundamentalism itself. Objections to the cross-cultural use of *fundamentalism* also demanded a convincing response. Critics maintained that the term referred exclusively to evangelical belief in millennialism and inerrant scripture. Imposing the label on communities outside the sphere of conservative Christianity, they insisted, not only violated the right of self-description but bordered on cultural imperialism as well. Another criticism asserted that the word had been so routinely and irresponsibly associated with allegations of extremism and violence that any communicative value once possessed by the term had been irretrievably lost.

Bruce Lawrence, a Yale-trained specialist in Islamic studies, met these challenges more effectively than any other author in the 1980s. The "word-purists," he argued, took a linguistically indefensible approach to the term and failed to recognize the technical potential within a renovated *fundamentalism*. At the same time, he admitted, advocates for a multicreedal application of the category ran the risk of committing the logical fallacy of erecting a typology of global fundamentalisms without going to the trouble of constructing a viable theory of fundamentalism congruent with the facts of cultural experience.[9]

Lawrence's achievement in comparative studies paralleled Marsden's in Protestant fundamentalism research. His analyses of case studies in Protestantism, Judaism, and Islam richly supplemented data gathered by predecessors, colleagues, and competitors. His main contribution to the enterprise was a conceptual model of fundamentalism set against the horizon of then fashionable theories of modernity, secularization, hermeneutics, paradigm formation, and cultural revitalization associated with thinkers such as Hans-Georg Gadamer, Thomas Kuhn, George Steiner, and Edward Shils. According to Lawrence, the "multifocal" phenomenon called fundamentalism is not necessarily linked to discrete criteria such as scriptural literalism, antievolution creationism, or apocalyptic expectation. Rather, it represents a new "religious ideology in multiple contexts." Specifically, he maintained, it is a critical, vigorous, inventive, and unprecedented counternarrative to the "text" of what historian Marshall Hodgson in his magnum opus *The Venture of Islam* (1977) christened the "Great Western Transmutation"—the set of historical processes that established secular Western hegemony in political, economic, and cultural spheres around the world. From Lawrence's perspective, fundamentalism is a multifaceted, idea-driven backlash against a "global pattern of change" in metaphysics and culture that profoundly marginalized religion in late modern, technological society.[10]

Lawrence's definition of this post-Enlightenment reactionary ideology constituted the most cogent and fully substantiated explanation of fundamentalism composed before the publication of the Fundamentalism Project volumes in the 1990s. *"Fundamentalism,"* he wrote, "is the affirmation of religious authority as holistic and absolute, admitting of neither criticism nor reduction; it is expressed through the collective demand that specific creedal and ethical dictates derived from scripture be publicly recognized and legally enforced." Borrowing Wittgenstein's trope of "family resemblances," destined to be the organizing principle of the Fundamentalism Project, he identified five basic traits that separate fundamentalist ideology from modernist opposition and nonfundamentalist faith: (1) an ingrained minority perspective, (2) an aggressively oppositional stance, (3) the non-negotiable authority of male elites, (4) an insider-only technical vocabulary, and (5) a recent point of historical origin associated with the rise of a sense of crisis in late modern experience.[11]

After Lawrence, motifs of militant activism, strategic anti-modernism, reinscribed patriarchy, and ironic identification with modernity—already well established in the scholarly profile of Christian fundamentalisms—became standard components of the academy's comparative vision of global fundamentalisms. They provided thematic structure for future studies such as Roger Stump's *Boundaries of Faith* (2000), Steve Bruce's *Fundamentalism* (2000), and Richard Antoun's *Understanding Fundamentalism* (2001), as well as popular treatments such as Karen

Armstrong's bestselling *The Battle for God* (2000) and Malise Ruthven's *Fundamentalism: The Search for Meaning* (2004).[12]

The Fundamentalism Project

The trend was most clearly seen in the volumes of the critically acclaimed Fundamentalism Project, the apex of twentieth-century fundamentalism studies. Briefly introduced in the previous chapter, the Fundamentalism Project was initiated in 1988 as a long-range, interdisciplinary undertaking commissioned by the American Academy of Arts and Sciences and funded by the John D. and Catherine T. MacArthur Foundation. Directed by Martin Marty and Scott Appleby, it engaged over two hundred scholars and religious leaders from a wide variety of traditions and cultures in a series of public conferences designed to submit the nature, history, scope, and significance of antisecular movements in all world religions to the full scrutiny of contemporary academic perspectives and procedures.

The tangible result of the project was a set of five mammoth volumes that came to be seen as the iconic emblem of the immensity of the enterprise and the weightiness and timeliness of its subject matter. The inaugural volume *Fundamentalisms Observed* (1991) focused on test cases from Protestantism, Catholicism, Judaism, Islam, Hinduism, Sikhism, Buddhism, Confucianism, and Japanese religions. *Fundamentalisms and Society* (1993) and *Fundamentalisms and the State* (1993) concentrated on fundamentalist attitudes toward science, education, gender, marriage, family, politics, economics, and violence. *Accounting for Fundamentalisms* (1994) analyzed the sources and dynamics of specific fundamentalist groups and movements. The final volume, *Fundamentalisms Comprehended* (1995), offered a methodological framework for the evolving study of fundamentalisms.[13]

Supplementary works issued from the project's élan, too. Marty and Appleby's *The Glory and the Power* (1992), a companion to public television and radio documentaries on world fundamentalisms, articulated an early exposition of the project's thesis for a general audience.[14] *Strong Religion* (2003), coauthored by Appleby and project veterans political scientist Gabriel Almond and historian Emmanuel Sivan, revisited the series' conclusions in the wake of the September 11, 2001, terrorist attacks on the Pentagon and World Trade Center. Functioning as a capstone to the nearly fifteen-year-long exercise in collaborative scholarship, the book made a compelling case for the cross-confessional application of *fundamentalism*, arguing that it ought to be compared to other abstract analytic categories in the scholarly repertoire, such as *nationalism, conservatism,* and *liberalism.*[15]

As we have seen, the unifying factor for the project was the conceit of "family resemblances," a notion rooted in Ludwig Wittgenstein's mature reflections on the structure and function of language. In the posthumously published *Philosophical Investigations* (1953), Wittgenstein explored the semantic field of "language games" and the larger field of "games" itself. "What is common to them all?" he asked.

> Don't say: "There *must* be something common, or they would not be called 'games'"—but *look* and *see* whether there is anything common to all.—For if you look at them you will not see something that is common to all, but similarities, relationships, and a whole series of them at that. To repeat: don't think, but look![16]

Wittgenstein was most interested in the way that rational analysis and intuitive insight cooperated in a single mental operation to recognize a common kind of reality uniting a wide range of empirical data. Surveying various types of games, he noticed how characteristics such as competition, amusement, chance, and score-keeping regularly appeared. He also noted that "similarities crop up and disappear." No single element or set of criteria, he observed, emerged as the determining factor that identified an

activity as a game. What he discovered instead was "a compli-
cated network of similarities overlapping and criss-crossing:
sometimes overall similarities, sometimes similarities of detail."[17]

In order to illuminate this common but sophisticated practice of perceiving such relational patterns in the complexity of
everyday life, Wittgenstein introduced into his discourse the idea
of "family resemblances" *(Familienähnlichkeiten):* "I can think
of no better expression to characterize these similarities than
'family resemblances'; for the various resemblances between
members of a family: build, features, colour of eyes, gait, tem-
perament, etc. etc. overlap and criss-cross in the same way.—And
I shall say: 'games' form a family."[18]

By seeking to "look and see" in this spirit, the Fundamentalism Project advanced the study of a vast number of organizations
and movements around the world. Its enduring contribution was
its investment of human, institutional, and financial resources
into sustained, critical reflection on the legitimacy and utility of
fundamentalism as a technical tool for uncovering some of the
"overlapping and criss-crossing" patterns embedded in the gram-
mar or gene pool of modern religion. From the first volume's
"Interim Report on a Hypothetical Family" to the final volume's
essay on "Fundamentalism: Genus and Species," a self-conscious
sensitivity to theory and method permeated the ethos of the entire
project. Although the project took on something of the character
of a mini-ecumenical council, neither the directors nor the participants assumed the mantle of infallibility; dissenting voices
gained a hearing within the pages of the official publications. As a
natural history of fundamentalisms, the project also avoided partisan theological judgment. Each volume's introductory and concluding sections reiterated the provisional character of the project
and the tentative quality of its findings.

A working consensus did emerge, however. The closing
essays in *Fundamentalisms Comprehended* confirmed the general
thrust of the original hypothesis—that the "comparative construct" of fundamentalism threw into relief what were previously

unaccountable phenomena on the world's religious landscape. According to the project collaborators, a rising tide of resistance to some of the most salient features of the modernizing process could be detected in diverse religious traditions and geographical areas—so much so that conventional boundaries of religious identity had to be redrawn and longstanding indicators of religious affiliation could no longer be relied upon to describe accurately the spirituality of people radicalized by perceived crises in modern experience.

What the project eventually pointed to, as the authors of *Strong Religion* maintained, was *"a discernible pattern of religious militance"* taking shape across religious and cultural lines.[19] The volumes of the Fundamentalism Project collectively and cumulatively argued that more and more "beleaguered believers"— "angry" Christians, Muslims, Jews, and, perhaps, Sikhs, Hindus, and Buddhists, too—were intentionally responding to perceived threats from the modern world in astonishingly similar ways. Some took aim at the modern nation-state's alleged hostility to religious values. Others lamented what they called the colonizing effect of modern science's "disenchanted" or desacralized worldview. Still others rallied to defend themselves against what appeared to be the assault of the secular West's cultural juggernaut. All confronted modernity with an intriguing blend of nostalgia and originality.

In so far as they attempted to (1) protect the purity of their worldview and their sacred enclave, (2) provoke symbolic and, when necessary, real confrontation with secular forces and apostate coreligionists, and (3) invent new ways to reinforce absolute fidelity to selected perennial truths and venerable practices in a godless age, the Fundamentalism Project ultimately suggested, these individuals from disparate faiths and disconnected lands shared a strangely familial perspective on world events that could best be described as fundamentalist. Participants in the Fundamentalism Project endeavored to make manifest the cognitive,

affective, and behavioral bonds that constituted a virtual fellowship of spiritual resentment in contemporary life.[20]

In the end, however, Marty and Appleby did not stake
everything on what Wittgenstein recognized as the bewitching
power of semantics. After scores of articles and nearly four thousand pages of text, pragmatic issues of measurement and prediction won the last word. In the final volume, the project directors
offered this conclusion:

> The fundamentalizing process, shared by otherwise quite
> different religiously inspired protest movements, will con-
> tinue to exist; and a knowledge of its dynamics will con-
> tinue to be essential to informed discussion of global
> religiopolitical resurgence, even if the term *fundamentalism*
> itself fades from the discourse of journalists, scholars, and
> diplomats.[21]

Discovering Islamic Fundamentalisms

One of the strengths of the Fundamentalism Project was its
keen interest in the Islamic tradition. Muslim scholars and non-
Muslim scholars of Islam played significant roles in the conference deliberations. Islamic intellectuals, activists, groups, and
movements provided the focus for numerous articles in the five
volumes. Islam itself routinely functioned as the test case for con-
tributors experimenting with a redefined *fundamentalism*. Even
in this context, however, there was never unanimity on the appro-
priateness of the term *Islamic fundamentalism*.

The first known reference to anything resembling *Islamic
fundamentalism* comes from the private correspondence of Sir
Reader Bullard, a legendary figure in British diplomatic history.
During the 1920s and 1930s, Bullard served as consul in Jeddah,
the chief entrance to the Arabian peninsula for pilgrims en route
to the holy cities Mecca and Medina. In a 1937 letter to his wife,
he commented on the tendency of Abd al-Aziz ibn al-Rahman

al-Saud, founder and first king of present-day Saudi Arabia, to find fault with subjects who adopted Western values, dress, and manners. "Ibn Saud," Bullard wrote, "has been coming out strong as a fundamentalist. Just before he left Mecca for Nejd…he published a proclamation criticising on religious grounds the Saudi young men who want modernization, freedom, progress, civilization, and the like. He was particularly fierce about women who mix with men under the cloak of progress, and neglect their proper role of wife and mother and housekeeper."[22] Historians have long confirmed the significance of Ibn Saud's alliance with the so-called Wahhabi movement, a reform impulse within Arabian Islam well known for its preoccupation with strict monotheism, its rigorous moral agenda, and its opposition to popular practices allegedly bordering on syncretism and idolatry. Unfortunately, nowhere in his writings did Bullard provide a clue as to why he chose the word *fundamentalist* to describe the Saudi monarch or his religious preferences.

The first author to employ *Islamic fundamentalism* in a published work was Sir Hamilton A. R. Gibb, whose service to Harvard's Center for Middle Eastern Studies during the 1950s and 1960s earned him a reputation as one of the Western world's leading Arabists. Gibb wrote in a context vastly different from Bullard's. The colonial empire that Bullard labored to maintain was breaking up. The birth of Pakistan and other independent Muslim nations suggested that Islam, after a century of forced hibernation, was on the verge of dramatic, global arousal. At the same time, Billy Graham's triumphs in Los Angeles, London, and Boston—not too far from Harvard Yard—demonstrated to an incredulous modern world that (Christian) fundamentalism was a force to be reckoned with.

Perhaps awareness of these events shaped Gibb's perceptions of Islam as a world-historical movement with an unscripted future. In *Mohammedanism* (1949, 1953), he located the preconditions for the postwar Islamic resurgence in the wave of resentment and self-doubt that swept the Muslim world during the nineteenth century. As Western powers competed for hegemony in what would later be called the Third World, Muslims from North Africa to South Asia fixated on the problem of Islam's "political weakness." Gibb suggested that the leaders who surfaced out of that mix of soul-searching and indignation were forerunners of the postcolonial Islamic renaissance coming to pass in his own day. He was especially interested in the way that Sayyid Jamal al-Din (better known as al-Afghani) set the pattern for the twentieth-century Muslim activist. Radicalized by the 1857 Indian Mutiny against the British *raj,* Afghani committed himself to the reinvigoration of Islamic solidarity and the defeat of Western imperialism. Though Afghani failed to achieve his dream of a pan-Islamic civilization raised on the best of modern knowledge and the riches of Islamic wisdom, he "lives on in the more recent popular movements which combine Islamic fundamentalism with an activist political programme," Gibb stated.[23]

Like Bullard before him, Gibb neither defined his terms nor explained his word choice. Nevertheless, injection of *fundamentalism* into an analysis of contemporary Islamic experience signaled a turning point in Middle Eastern historiography and fundamentalism studies. After his death in 1971, countless writers would follow Gibb's lead, the vast majority largely ignorant of his precedence.

One of the first scholars fully to appropriate the new terminology was historian R. Stephen Humphreys. A Princeton research fellow at the time, Humphreys now holds the King Abdul Aziz Ibn Saud chair at the University of California, Santa Barbara. In a 1979 *Middle East Journal* article investigating the contemporary political ferment in Saudi Arabia, Egypt, and Syria, he identified fundamentalism as one of the three viable intellectual options for the engaged Muslim in a postcolonial age. The other two options, he said, were secularism and modernism. His approach to fundamentalism, anticipating key directions in fundamentalism studies for the next several years, accented fundamentalism's distance from ordinary orthodoxy, its appeal to educated classes, and its unique fusion of tradition and novelty. "We may define Fundamentalism," Humphreys wrote,

> as the reaffirmation, in a radically changed environment, of traditional modes of understanding and behavior. In contrast to conservatism or traditionalism, which assumes that things can and should go on much as they have for genera-tions past, Fundamentalism recognizes and tries to speak to a changed milieu, an altered atmosphere of expectations. Fundamentalism is by no means a blind opponent of all social change, but it insists that change must be governed by traditional values and modes of understanding.[24]

By the 1980s, *Islamic fundamentalism*—not always paired with the precision of Humphrey's prose—had acquired an inter-national vogue. Many Muslims adopted it along with its unchecked interreligious connotations. Neologisms appeared in Arabic and Farsi. *Salafi* and *usuli* communicated the literal sense of "one who adheres to fundamentals or roots," and *al-usuliyyah al-Islamiyyah* rendered verbatim the nearly ubiquitous *Islamic fundamentalism*. Some supporters of Ayatollah Khomeini intro-duced a similarly literal noun *bonyadegar* in Iran.[25]

Fundamentalism, however, has never gained general accep-tance in the worldwide Islamic community. Specialists in Islamic studies, some only minimally acquainted with developments in Christian fundamentalism studies, have pointed out that literal interpretation of scripture (erroneously thought to be the essence of fundamentalism) is not actually one of the identifying features of putative fundamentalist movements among Muslims. Some Muslim critics, unwilling to surrender theological high ground, have objected to the word, claiming it implies that nonfundamen-talist Muslims disregard the fundamentals of Islamic belief and practice. Many Muslim intellectuals have rejected the term as a not-so-subtle expression of cultural imperialism. Cambridge anthropologist Akbar Ahmed has dubbed *fundamentalism* the "bogeyman" of the West.[26]

Today most scholars of Islam recognize the achievements of the Fundamentalism Project and comparable research efforts. Many accept *fundamentalism* as a neutral, descriptive rubric for the critical study of one slice of contemporary religion. Feminist scholar Haideh Moghissi has judged it to be superior to its alternatives.[27] Political scientist Roxanne Euben has called it "a useful heuristic device," if not pushed too far. Other scholars grudgingly concede the place of the "slippery label" in academic discourse but continue to underscore its problematic nature.[28] Georgetown University's John Esposito spoke for many when he declared that *Islamic fundamentalism* "tells us everything and yet, at the same time, nothing." Some experts agree with Johannes Jansen's verdict on the "infertile" quality of the seemingly undying debate over the category's extra-Christian legitimacy. "In any case," as Iranian-born philosopher Seyyed Hossein Nasr has observed, "the unfortunate use of the term 'fundamentalism'…for Islam cannot now be avoided, but it is of the utmost importance to realize that it embraces very different phenomena and must not be confused with the demonizing usage of the term in the Western media." Proposed alternatives for *Islamic fundamentalism* include *political Islam, radical Islam,* and *revolutionary Islam.* Only *Islamism* and its companion term *Islamist* have secured anything close to broad approval.[29]

The Islamic Revival and Islamism

The linguistic controversy aside, all contemporary observers of modern Islam agree on three crucial points. First, before World War II, the House of Islam was in disrepair if not decay. Since the Ottoman Empire's failure to penetrate the heart of Christian Europe in the seventeenth century and Napoleon's invasion of Egypt just a hundred years later, Islamic civilization had been in an agonizing process of deterioration, especially in contrast to the rising fortunes of the post-Renaissance Christian West. Second, after World War II,

Islam began to reassert itself on the world stage. In recent decades, Muslim intellectuals and activists have sought to reenergize Islamic identity through reclamation of the tradition's core values, reconnection with its glorious past, and resistance to forces that would denigrate it or divert it from its world-historical destiny.

Third, the leading edge of the postwar Islamic Revival, as it is now generally known, has been a variant of modern Islam unusually militant in its orientation and doubly alarmed by the external threat of a decadent but still imperialist West and the internal danger of a complacent or even apostate Islam. Distinct from other modes of Islamic tradition, the aggressive wing of the Islamic Revival—whatever its appropriate appellation—represents a remarkable development within the Muslim world. For several decades, politically astute and technologically savvy reform movements—often virtuosic in modern methods of organization and persuasion, yet vehemently opposed to the cultural and moral fruits of modernity—have been radically transforming the face of international Islam.

John Esposito, founding director of Georgetown's Center for Muslim-Christian Understanding and editor of major reference works on Islam such as *The Oxford History of Islam* (2000) and *The Oxford Dictionary of Islam* (2003), has written extensively on the Islamic Revival, often with a non-Muslim audience in mind. In numerous publications, he has described the Revival as "a vibrant, multifaceted movement" reinvigorating spiritual and corporate life in all quarters of the transnational Islamic family.[30] With historians Yvonne Yazbeck Haddad and John O. Voll, he has produced the definitive works on the literature of and about the Islamic Revival: *The Contemporary Islamic Revival* (1991) and *The Islamic Revival Since 1988* (1997).[31]

For Esposito, the Islamic Revival represents nothing less than the "dominant theme of contemporary Islam." Its worldview, he maintains, can be reduced to six major principles: (1) belief in Islam as a "comprehensive way of life," integral to every dimension of existence; (2) self-criticism of the Muslim world's abandonment of

the "straight path" of Islam for the seductive "secular path" of
Western materialism; (3) renewal of Muslim society through re-
Islamization of religious and cultural identity; (4) replacement of
Western civil codes with divinely ordained law, or *Sharia;* (5) subor-
dination of modern science and technology to Islamic standards of
belief and ethics; and (6) willingness to engage in jihad (struggle)
against forces of injustice and unbelief.[32]

Tighten the theological screw, Esposito has suggested, and
the Revival's worldview crystallizes into the intense vision of
Islamism or Islamic fundamentalism. He portrays the groups and
movements fostered by this outlook as galvanized by the conviction that the present epoch in global history represents a "Muslim
moment" pregnant with opportunities for a universal faith yet
fraught with hazards for a community devoted to supernatural revelation. In *The Islamic Threat: Myth or Reality?* (1992, 1999),
Esposito characterized Islamism as a passionate reaction to the
social and intellectual challenges emanating from the post-
Enlightenment processes of modernization, Westernization, and
globalization. From the Islamist perspective, he has explained, the
fate of Islam's dream of revitalization hinges on the ability of dedicated Muslims to respond decisively to three principal threats:
(1) the "Crusader mentality" of Western powers, (2) a "Judeo-
Christian conspiracy" jeopardizing Muslim faith, and (3) the ille-
gitimacy of Muslim governments co-opted by Western culture.[33]

The first threat, often seen as bent on cultural genocide,
takes multiple forms in Islamist consciousness. Christian missions and the mass media's effort to impose a normative mono-
culture on other countries stem from a messianic impulse latent in
Western civilization and a legacy of anti-Islamic sentiment reach-
ing back through Voltaire and Dante to the eighth century's John
of Damascus. Economic exploitation of Third World markets and
superpower colonial ambitions issue from even less altruistic currents in the Western soul. All of these threats, according to the
Islamist vision of reality, are rooted in the West's deeply
ingrained ethnocentrism and "Islamaphobia."

The second threat identified by Esposito looms especially large in the Islamist imagination: Western, particularly American, support for Zionism and the nation-state of Israel. The 1948 establishment of a Jewish state on Palestinian soil continues to strike millions of Muslims as a glaring injustice of modern experience. Collective memory of the "disaster" of Israel's capture of Sinai, the Golan Heights, Gaza, the West Bank, East Jerusalem, and Al-Haram al-Sharif (the Temple Mount) during the 1967 Six Day War persistently breeds bitterness in the Muslim soul and reinforces a visceral sense of political despair. The plight of the Palestinian people has fueled Islamic fundamentalisms perhaps more than any other issue. Since the 1980s, the Palestinian *intifada* (uprising) against Israel has served as an archetype for popular Islamic resistance movements in many regions around the globe.

The third threat perceived by Muslim fundamentalists, according to Esposito, comes from within the Islamic household itself. Like the Kharijite sect of early Islam, which staked everything on separating authentic from counterfeit Muslims, contemporary Islamist movements operate on the assumption that not everyone claiming Islamic credentials is necessarily a true Muslim. Nor is the leadership of the Muslim community exempt from Islamism's critical eye. According to some fundamentalist movements, pragmatic political rulers and jaded religious authorities have so corrupted the faith with alien political theories or materialism, based on oil wealth, that they deserve to be classed with unbelievers and are themselves legitimate targets of jihad—struggle in the form of intellectual critique or violent opposition through armed rebellion. Much of the malaise haunting modern Islam, they assert, is directly attributable to elites who have squandered Islam's spiritual birthright. Such sentiment led to revolt against the Shah of Iran and assassination of Egyptian president Anwar Sadat. One of the hallmarks of the Islamist adaptation of the Islamic Revival is an understanding of jihad as a moral imperative directing the Muslim into combat on two fronts. Striving to rid the faith of inner impurities and defend it against external adversaries, fundamentalists contend, is the urgent task of every devout Muslim in the crisis of the present hour.

Esposito's *Islamic Threat* situated the Islamic Revival and Islamism in the context of longstanding rivalry with Western culture and the history of the Muslim community's variegated responses to the Western-generated phenomenon of modernity. Most of the comparativists mentioned in the first two sections of this chapter followed a similar tack as they addressed Islamic issues. For them, Islamic fundamentalism is best understood as first and foremost the product of a unique interchange with modernity. What distinguishes Islamic fundamentalism from the North American Protestant prototype is the peculiar angle of its contact with things modern. As modern Westerners themselves, first-wave Protestant fundamentalists had few quarrels with modern inventions such as representative government, capitalism, or early Enlightenment science; they attacked modernism, secularism, the sexual revolution, and "Second Enlightenment" science because of preconceived ideas regarding the proper Christian course of their own culture. Muslim fundamentalists, on the other hand, have experienced modernity as a Western export—foreign cultural cargo associated with technological brilliance and unimaginable wealth but also linked to a record of colonial aggression and seemingly a growing propensity for impiety.

A contrasting approach, adopted by a minority of scholars, has attempted to understand Islamic revivalism and fundamentalism as developments occurring naturally within the dynamics of Islamic intellectual life. Before his death in 1988, University of Chicago scholar Fazlur Rahman initiated a project to trace the cycles of decline and revival in Muslim spirituality from the emergence of Sunni orthodoxy and countervailing mystical alternatives to the rise of twentieth-century "neo-fundamentalism"—a term he used to emphasize modern fundamentalism's continuities with a long tradition of debate and reflection. His posthumous *Revival and Reform in Islam: A Study of Islamic Fundamentalism* (2000) brought the narrative forward only as far as Indian reformist thought at the dawn of the second Muslim millennium.[34]

Historian John Voll, Esposito's colleague at Georgetown, has pursued a comparable research agenda. *Islam: Continuity and Change in the Modern World* (1982, 1994) and a spate of essays since the 1980s, including the entry on "Fundamentalism" for *The Oxford Encyclopedia of the Modern Islamic World* (1995), have contributed to a distinctively organic interpretation of Islamic fundamentalism.[35] Voll's Islamocentric model seeks to explain fundamentalism primarily in terms of categories drawn from the Muslim heritage itself. All dimensions of the contemporary Islamic Revival, including fundamentalist trajectories, he has argued, have deep roots in the tradition's patterns of *tajdid* (renewal) and *islah* (reform). Islamic theology, like its Jewish and Christian counterparts, has passed through phases of experimentation, consolidation, disintegration, and rediscovery. Despite canonical commitment to a linear view of time and Muhammad's position at the culmination of prophecy, some Muslim thinkers have seen their tradition as vulnerable to periodic slips into states of degeneration comparable to the mythic "age of ignorance" *(jahiliyya)* that preceded the Prophet's call. The Muslim's duty in such circumstances, they insist, is to engage in prophetic critique of the status quo—recapitulating in a sense the original mission of Muhammad. Islam's "*tajdid-islah* tradition has never been a static one," Voll wrote in *Voices of Resurgent Islam* (1983). "The significant expressions of this tradition that are most readily available to contemporary Muslims," he said, "are those that are currently called 'fundamentalist.'"[36]

An eye for continuity brings with it an interest in genealogy. Historians intent on reconstructing the lineage of fundamentalism have focused especially on the individuals who laid the foundations for contemporary Islamic fundamentalist thought and practice. Scholarly consensus identifies a handful of formative figures: (1) Muhammad Ibn Abd al-Wahhab, the eighteenth-century Arabian reformer whose pristine "Wahhabi" Islam gained the patronage of the Saudi royals—and later, the endorsement of anti-Saudi tycoon-terrorist Osama bin Laden; (2) Hasan al-Banna, the charismatic Egyptian educator whose anti-imperialist Muslim Brotherhood (founded in 1928) fostered a blend of political opposition, clandestine activism, and Islamic self-help to counteract the "slow annihilation" of Muslim society through Westernization; (3) Indian journalist Sayyid Abu'l-A'la Mawdudi, founder of the Jama'at-i-Islami (Islamic Party), who broke with the Gandhian independence movement to promote a separate Muslim homeland based on "theodemocracy" and, after the 1947 partition of the subcontinent, campaigned for the full Islamization of Pakistan; and (4) Iran's Ayatollah Khomeini, "the first man in modern times," as historian Lawrence Davidson has noted, "to successfully realize the establishment of a revolutionary Islamic state."[37] Some scholars cite medieval Syrian mystic and jurist Ibn Taymiyah as a distant ancestor of contemporary fundamentalists. His defense of jihad against both non-Muslims and uncommitted Muslims has been appropriated by numerous apologists for jihad in the modern context.[38]

Pride of place in the roster, though, is usually given to Muslim Brotherhood man of letters Sayyid Qutb, described by many observers as the spiritual father of Islamic fundamentalism and, in light of his execution by President Nasser's government in 1966, a martyr for the cause of the Islamic Revival. Narratives of Qutb's biography rehearse the story of a conventional intellectual life radically redirected by dissatisfaction with the Arab world's ineffective response to European imperialism. A study tour of the United States after World War II convinced him that the modern West's material prosperity masked only a fraction of its profound spiritual bankruptcy. His cultural criticism of the 1950s and 1960s portrayed the West as a decadent civilization ruined by commercialism, racism, hedonism, and a "hideous schizophrenia" that divorced faith from public life.[39] His theological works presented Islam as the only remedy for such spiritual and social maladies — a "universal declaration of human liberation" that restored all of life to integrity under the will of God. His masterpiece *Ma'alim fi al-Tariq* (*Milestones,* 1964), written during a ten-year prison sentence, summoned modern Muslims to resist both the West's "*jahili* society" and Muslim regimes that had reverted to pre-Islamic *jahiliyya*. Resistance, he explained, could take the form of the jihad of "admonition" or, when necessary, the jihad of the "sword." The aim of the book, Qutb stated, was to provide "signposts" for a "vanguard" of committed Muslims who would set in motion a worldwide Islamic resurrection.[40]

Called the "manifesto" of the Islamist movement, Qutb's *Milestones* has since the 1960s inspired diverse sectors of the Islamic population. Gilles Kepel's *Muslim Extremism in Egypt* (1985) drew a straight line from the book to the Egyptian military officers who assassinated "Pharaoh" Sadat in 1981. More recently, Qutb's thought has enjoyed a renaissance among mainstream Western Muslims worried about the erosion of religious values in an atmosphere saturated with moral relativism. The on-line version of *Milestones* delivers the rationale for resurgence to a new generation of alienated Muslim youth. Qutb's message also resonates with a fresh "vanguard" of radical Muslims spread throughout the world in a variety of separatist movements seeking physical isolation or cognitive insulation from modern culture and guerrilla networks mobilizing for a violent overthrow of "infidel" Western powers and their Third World clients. In *Jihad* (2002), Kepel extended the line of his own argument, linking Qutb's legacy directly to Osama bin Laden, who studied with the apologist's brother Muhammad at Jeddah's Abdul Aziz University.[41]

Islamism After 9/11

The 9/11 attacks of 2001 pushed Islamic fundamentalism studies to new levels of intensity and relevance. As hijacked jumbo jets crashed into the World Trade Center and the Pentagon, icons for much of the world of American materialism and militarism, students of the fundamentalist impulse in Islam witnessed the public realization of their worst fears. In an eerie replay of their reaction to the "shock" of the Iranian Revolution two decades earlier, journalists scrambled to comprehend the "how" and the "why" of the horrific events. Anti-Islamic critics and conspiracy theorists refurbished old polemics and apocalyptic fantasies. Anglo-American power brokers read the events through the lens of Samuel Huntington's "clash of civilizations" paradigm and initiated a global "war on terror" that ironically divided the West against itself.[42] Responses from the Islamic world ranged from moral repudiation of the attacks and the "misled Muslims" who executed them to calls for redoubled anti-Western defiance, especially in light of the subsequent American-led invasion and occupation of Iraq.[43] In *The Clash of Fundamentalisms* (2002), Pakistani author Tariq Ali turned the tables on Western moralism, condemning U.S. imperialism as the "mother of all fundamentalisms."[44]

Scholars responded to the 9/11 tragedy by reviewing the entire series of arguments that had been advanced since Sir Reader Bullard detected something queer in Ibn Saud's penchant for Arabian puritanism. Comparativists perceived in the events ugly confirmation of their thesis. Historians probed the "roots of Muslim rage" with renewed determination.[45] No one failed to notice the diabolical mix of medieval and modern in the events, as cutting-edge aeronautics and computer technology transformed ancient jihad into "spectacular terrorism."[46]

Since 9/11, and similar strikes on public targets in Mombasa, Riyadh, Casablanca, Jakarta, Madrid, Amman, London, and Mumbai, scholars of Islamic fundamentalism have worked diligently to understand the world's new season of Muslim fury. Looking for signposts of their own, they continue to scour every dimension of Islamist discontent in the world's vast Qur'an Belt—from Morocco to Malaysia. Many have focused on the ongoing insurgency in Iraq, the survival of Taliban forces in Afghanistan, the nuclear ambitions of Iran, and the fortunes of the militant Hamas Party after its landslide victory in the Palestinian Authority elections of 2006. An increasing number of scholars monitor the new frontiers of immigrant Islam in Western nations and of virtual Islam in cyberspace. The fruits of Muslim rage, however, remain unpredictable.

6
Comparative Fundamentalism Studies: Judaism and Asian Religions

The Islamist wing of the international Islamic Revival provided the original test case for the comparative study of global fundamentalisms. Most of the scholars experimenting with a redefined *fundamentalism* during the 1980s and 1990s were either specialists in Islamic studies with competence in Christianity or specialists in Christian studies with competence in Islamic history. Judaism, it often seemed, entered the conversation mainly for reasons of Abrahamic symmetry. Hypotheses regarding fundamentalist trends in religions outside the Abrahamic trio of Judaism, Christianity, and Islam also surfaced in the literature during this period, but to this day they remain the most disputed questions of the entire academic enterprise.

This chapter completes our survey of recent trends in comparative fundamentalism scholarship. It explores the main issues involved in the investigation of countermodern movements transforming Judaism and indigenous traditions of Asia: Hinduism, Sikhism, and Buddhism. Like Protestants and Catholics, Jews have not been immune to the dislocations of modernity or the uncertainties of post-Enlightenment experience. Their minority status within Western culture and their unique relationship to the nation-state of Israel, however, have distinctively shaped the ways in which they have reacted to and even perceived the challenges of modernity. Perhaps more than any other factor, the traditional Jewish emphasis on practice rather than doctrine has accounted for the contrast between Jewish evaluations of secular modernity and those characteristic of the Protestant fundamentalist outlook.

Members of traditional Asian religions, too, have generated a unique set of responses to modernity's world and worldview. Like Muslims, however, Hindus, Sikhs, and Buddhists have encountered modernity principally through experiences of Western imperialism, colonial occupation, and cultural globalization—phenomena that, in many instances, have retained at least traces of an ethnocentric, triumphalist Christian vision. Is there evidence to suggest that practitioners of some of the world's oldest faiths are now making their own mark on the axis of sacred rebellion first erected by "angry" American evangelicals in the twentieth century? Researchers in comparative fundamentalism studies are currently pursuing this very question and others related to it. The next phase of the academic study of fundamentalism will most likely be characterized by even greater emphasis on non-Christian and non-Islamic expressions of religious antimodernism.

Jewish Separatism

The first references to a Jewish form of fundamentalism appeared alongside the initial revisionist experiments in Christian and Muslim studies published after the neo-fundamentalist renaissance of the 1970s. Lionel Caplan's *Studies in Religious Fundamentalism* (1987), the book that set the pace for all future comparative ventures in fundamentalism research, devoted one chapter to Jewish topics and established what would become a resilient Christian-Muslim-Jewish scheme. Bruce Lawrence,

Gilles Kepel, Karen Armstrong, Richard Antoun, and numerous other writers followed suit. Of the nearly one hundred articles filling the five volumes of the Fundamentalism Project, less than a tenth dealt exclusively with issues related to Jewish life and thought. Virtually every comparative treatment of fundamentalism since the 1990s has addressed Judaism in one way or another, but today the critical literature still contains only a handful of monographs on the question of Jewish fundamentalisms.

The low scholarly turnout on the subject reflects the contentious debate on fundamentalism within the discipline of Jewish studies. Jonathan Webber, author of the essay on Judaism in Caplan's book, all but dismissed "Jewish fundamentalism," calling it no more than a "convenient shorthand." In the 1992 *Concilium* issue on "Fundamentalism as an Ecumenical Challenge," Jacob Neusner, dean of Jewish studies in America, went on record declaring *fundamentalism* to be a "questionable term" in reference to Jewish experience.[1] Criticisms of what opponents see as a cookie-cutter approach to the category mirror the objections raised by Muslim intellectuals and Islamic scholars concerned about cultural imperialism and the distortion of evidence for the sake of an ideological agenda. For some analysts, the very idea of Jewish fundamentalism constitutes an unwarranted "Protestantization" of the study of Judaism. In a seminal essay articulating these criticisms, historian Jay Harris reviewed standard criteria of fundamentalism—antimodernism, scriptural inerrancy, gender control, minority consciousness—and argued that all four factors effectively illuminate dynamics inside modern Judaism without the aid of a superimposed concept of fundamentalism.[2]

Scholars who employ the category of Jewish fundamentalism do so with varying levels of approval, ranging from reluctant toleration to principled acceptance. The groundbreaking essays on Judaism in *Fundamentalisms Observed* exemplified two different approaches. Samuel Heilman and Menachem Friedman described the world of far-right Haredi segregationists, more or less sidestepping the controversy over fundamentalism. By contrast,

Gideon Aran directly engaged the interpretive category in his analysis of radical religious Zionism in Israel, speaking suggestively of a "fundamentalist spark" at the heart of the movement.[3]

These two articles also represent the way in which journalists and academics have tended to choose between vastly different segments of world Jewry in their attempt to identify examples of a fundamentalist impulse within Judaism. Some writers—Kepel, Lawrence, Marty, Appleby, Nielsen, Israel Shahak, and Norton Mezvinsky, for example—have tried to make the case that both Haredi Jews and religious Zionists fall appropriately under the category of Jewish fundamentalism. The essays in Laurence Silberstein's edited volume *Jewish Fundamentalism in Comparative Perspective* (1993) exemplified this broad, inclusive approach.[4] For other writers, though, the hypothesis of a bipolar Jewish fundamentalism strains plausibility in the same way that squeezing Amish farmers and mega-church entrepreneurs into a "conservative Christian" pigeonhole discredits overly ambitious theoretical typologies for many students of the Christian experience. Some of these skeptics maintain that Judaism's only genuine fundamentalists are the religiously separatist Haredim, who adhere strictly to creeds and codes out of sync with modern values and painstakingly calculate every interaction with the secular world. Others argue that the real Jewish fundamentalists are in fact the zealous activists of right-wing Zionism, well known for their devotion to settlement ventures in Israel's occupied territories and their willingness to use violence against any party—non-Jewish or Jewish—that threatens to prevent Jews from attaining full possession of the biblical land of Israel.

The best introductions to the first class of putative Jewish fundamentalists are *Defenders of the Faith* (1992) by Queens College sociologist Samuel Heilman and *Piety and Power* (1993) by Israeli journalist David Landau.[5] Both authors relied upon ethnographic methods in order to penetrate, describe, and understand the mental and behavioral world of Haredi Jews. The term *Haredim* refers to a variety of groups making up the ultra-orthodox wing of Judaism. It derives from the ancient Hebrew meaning those who "tremble" before the word of God (Isa 66:5) and is often rendered "God-fearers." The Haredi movement originated as a negative reaction to the eighteenth-century Haskalah, the Jewish version of the Enlightenment that raised not only questions of biblical criticism and modern science but also hitherto unknown possibilities of cultural assimilation. The Haredi movement's roots reach back to three main sources: (1) classical rabbinic Judaism based on domestic ritual, synagogue worship, and the mythic worldview of the Talmud; (2) Hasidism, the pietist movement founded in eighteenth-century Poland by mystic Israel ben Eliezer (the Baal Shem Tov); and (3) Mitnagdism, the traditional rabbinic movement that originally disapproved of Hasidism for its alleged excesses of enthusiasm and anti-intellectualism but eventually became its loyal opposition in the multidimensional world of ultra-orthodox Judaism. While some Jews attempted to reconcile faith and practice with modern values, the Haredim, in all of their diversity, opposed assimilation and compromise with secularity.[6]

The chief feature of the Haredi movement today is rigorous observance of *halachah* (Jewish law). In contrast to modern forms of Orthodox Judaism, the Haredim are committed to unyielding separatism and a set of distinctive folkways inherited from the premodern culture of the eastern European Jewish *shtetl* (village)—not simply traditional dietary practices and prayer rituals, but public markers of collective identity such as attire, hairstyle, gender roles, and speech. Haredi Jews question the Jewish identity of Reform and Conservative Jews and converts. The Lubavitch or Habad sect of Hasidism actively proselytizes other Jews, encouraging them to return to traditional religious observance.

Since the Holocaust, the Haredim have existed in insular, countercultural communities in Israel, North America, and parts of western Europe. The most famous community is the Mea Shearim district of Jerusalem, well known for its ban on Sabbath Day automobile traffic and its "fashion police" who aggressively confront immodestly dressed tourists. Like other antimodernists, many Haredim have never wholly rejected the technological products of modern culture. Expert use of state-of-the-art electronic communication, as Landau has observed, makes the contemporary international world of the Haredim "a global shtetl."[7]

The present worldwide Haredi population is estimated at 500,000 to 700,000, and trends suggest future growth. Long known for political quietism, the Haredim in recent years have become more involved in partisan politics. In the United States, bloc voting supports candidates favoring federal funding for parochial schools. In Israel, Haredim have offered increasing support for conservative political parties. At the same time, many Haredim—especially Israel's Neturei Karta (Guardians of the City)—continue to reject secular and religious Zionisms. Some describe the state of Israel as "unholy," "anti-Jewish," even "Satanic." Some see the Holocaust as divine punishment for the "sin" of Zionist colonization. Convinced that only supernatural forces will fully restore the people of Israel and its ancient homeland, the Haredim believe that Zionism in any form violates three classic oaths imposed upon the Jewish people by God, as recorded in Talmudic and midrashic literature: oaths forswearing (1) Jewish rebellion against non-Jews, (2) mass emigration to Palestine before the advent of the Messiah, and (3) inordinately fervent prayer for the coming of the Messiah before his appointed time.[8]

Jewish Nationalism

For one set of observers, the Haredim constitute the true Jewish counterparts to Christian and Muslim fundamentalists by virtue of their commitment to cultural segregation, their absolute allegiance to rabbinic authority, and their scrupulous maintenance of cognitive and behavioral identity boundaries out of tune with modern norms. For others, it is precisely hard-core religious Zionism that represents Judaism's closest parallel to countermodern protest movements in other religions. At home in the modern world of scientific method and technological application, radical religious Zionists question the legitimacy of the secular nation-state and its privatization of religion, its promotion of cultural pluralism, and its penchant for political pragmatism. While other fundamentalists earnestly contend for the faith once delivered to the saints (the authority of holy creed or infallible canon), activists of religious Zionism reassert the ancient primacy of nation and land. With their providential view of history and a heterogeneous approach to geography, separating sacred from profane space in stark contrast to the secular city's homogeneous space, they create for themselves a unique niche in the global ecology of fundamentalisms.

Zionism is about as hotly contested a topic as fundamentalism itself. Its history remains one of the most understudied phenomena of modern times. Few treatments of the movement have escaped prejudice or partisan perspective. Classroom shorthand identifies modern or political Zionism as originally a secular movement, issuing from Viennese journalist Theodore Herzl's reaction to the infamous Dreyfus affair in France and the spread of a new intellectual virus of Jew-hatred throughout late nineteenth-century European society. Coined in 1879, the neologism *anti-Semitism* has over time come to be understood as the sign of a distinctively modern variant of anti-Jewish sentiment based on a post-Darwinian pseudo-science of race — not to be confused with the older, more theologically driven, anti-Judaism inherited by Western culture from the *adversos Judaeos* tradition of early Christian thought. Herzl's *The Jewish State* (1896), according to the standard narrative, aroused interest in a legally protected Jewish homeland principally among cosmopolitan Jews of the Haskalah who had benefited most from the modern processes of emancipation and assimilation and whose Jewishness consisted mainly in affiliation with a history of cultural experience rather than faithfulness to a religious vision or the practice of traditional cult and code.

In reality, however, Zionism has always included within its ranks Jews of secular orientations as well as representatives from every sector of religious Judaism. Labor socialists, agrarian reformers, and humanist Jews made significant contributions to the movement, but so did Orthodox activists, messianic enthusiasts, and independent thinkers such as philosopher Martin Buber, whose mystical "Hebrew Humanism" proposed Jewish nationalism as a prophetic alternative to other nationalisms tainted with the egoistic quest for power. Jacob Neusner once called Zionism "a peculiar marriage of Western romantic nationalism and Eastern Jewish piety."[9]

Observers who posit a fundamentalist element within rightwing Zionism have typically concentrated on the Israeli settler movement called Gush Emunim (Bloc of the Faithful). Studies of Gush Emunim began to appear in social science journals during the mid-1970s. David Newman's edited volume *The Impact of Gush Emunim* (1985), followed by Ehud Sprinzak's *Gush Emunim: The Politics of Zionist Fundamentalism in Israel* (1986) and Ian Lustick's *For the Land and the Lord* (1988), offered early arguments for the interpretation of the movement as a Jewish form of fundamentalism on par with Iran's revolutionary Islam and America's New Religious Right.[10] Gideon Aran's article in *Fundamentalisms Observed,* based on participant-observation fieldwork with the group during the 1980s, maintained that the heuristic value of the analogy between non-Jewish fundamentalisms and radical Zionism outweighed the understandable skepticism of scholars who questioned the very concept of Jewish fundamentalism.[11]

Gush Emunim was organized in 1974, the same year the United Nations declared Zionism to be racism and just a year after the Yom Kippur War forced Israel's partial withdrawal from land seized during the Six Day War (1967). It soon became the most aggressive and provocative form of religious Zionism in Israel since the country's founding in 1948. Flourishing from the mid-1970s to the mid-1980s, the group provided settlers in the territories of Judea, Samaria, the Gaza Strip, and the Golan Heights with an infrastructure and an ideology that promised to make their dream of a theocratic "Greater Israel" a political and geographical reality. Gush Emunim's vision of "redemptive Zionism" was based on the thought of Palestine's first chief rabbi Abraham Isaac Kook, his son Tzvi Yehudah Kook, and a disciple of Kook the Younger, Rabbi Moshe Levinger. The ideology fused the activism of secular Zionism with the messianic supernaturalism of holistic Orthodoxy. The result, according to Hebrew University sociologist Aran, was a "high-voltage religion" of race, real estate, and revenge appealing to "born-again Jews" who would participate in the historic "re-Judaization of Israel"—by whatever means necessary.[12]

The renowned "knitted skullcap culture" of Gush Emunim and related groups in the larger settler movement has revealed a familiar blend of bohemian cool, cyber chic, and back-to-the-land romanticism found among disenchanted and intellectually adventurous young people and their middle-aged mentors in virtually every society touched by both globalization and a sense of lost innocence and integrity. What has made some groups in the settler movement stand out on the Israeli landscape has been their tendency toward a frontier style of vigilante violence. Antagonistic toward Palestinian populations and surrounding Arab nations, more radical members of the movement have also been defiant toward what they see as a compromising Israeli government— always, from their point of view, at least ankle-deep in one or another program of self-defeating peace negotiations.

The trend toward terrorism in the Zionist underground has been exposed in a number of incidents since the early 1980s. Arguably the most dramatic involved core Gush Emunim members in a 1984 plot to blow up Al-Aqsa Mosque and the Dome of the Rock on East Jerusalem's ancient Temple Mount. Two other events, no less tragic, included American-born disciples of Rabbi Meir Kahane, founder of the Jewish Defense League and the notoriously chauvinist Kach Party. In 1982, Maryland native Alan

Goodman went on a forty-five-minute shooting spree in the Dome of the Rock. In 1994, Brooklyn-born physician Baruch Goldstein murdered twenty-nine Arabs during prayer services at the Tomb of the Patriarchs in Hebron. Yigal Amir, the Israeli law student who assassinated Prime Minister Yitzhak Rabin in 1995, confessed that Goldstein's actions inspired him to engage in his own act of "self-sacrifice" for the Zionist cause.[13]

The radical Zionist underground also hosts a curiously interfaith subculture obsessed with apocalyptic visions of a reconstructed temple and a restored priesthood. A cottage industry driven by this eschatological theology of history faithfully manufactures musical instruments, silver shekels, designer vestments, and altar vessels in anticipation of a reestablished sacrificial cult. Bible-reading cattlemen attempt to breed the "red heifer without spot" (Num 19:2) that they believe is required for the rites of the restored temple. In *The End of Days: Fundamentalism and the Struggle for the Temple Mount* (2000), Jerusalem-based editor Gershom Gorenberg illuminated this subterranean world where Christian Right and Jewish Right converge in mutually fulfilling fantasies of a second coming and a Third Temple. Timothy Weber's *On the Road to Armageddon* (2004) represents a new stream in Protestant historical scholarship, documenting American evangelicals' infatuation with Zionism, their uncritical support for the state of Israel, their eschatological interpretation of geopolitical events, and their commitment to the evangelization of Jews.[14] Bringing the comparative study of fundamentalisms full circle, these studies have provided intriguing grassroots evidence for "family resemblances" linking latter-day disciples of John Darby's premillennialism with the most recent kin of John the Baptist who would take the kingdom by force.

Today die-hard religious Zionists continue to view the Israeli government and official peace plans suspiciously. In 2005, some settlers resisted authorities as they constructed a highly controversial concrete and barbed-wire "security barrier" through sections of the occupied territories and executed equally controversial plans to dismantle and relocate pioneer communities. Defiant settlers in Gaza and the West Bank, some wearing yellow stars, burned eviction notices delivered to them by unarmed Israeli soldiers and police officers, while radical rabbis exhorted soldiers to disobey the government's "anti-Jewish" orders. One protestor set herself on fire to express her sense of outrage over the evacuation orders. Still, the government evacuated all of the Gaza settlements and a portion of the West Bank communities without serious violence, leaving the Zionist settler cause in a state of limbo. A year later, Israeli offensives into Gaza and renewed conflict between the Jewish state and Hezbollah militia in Lebanon cast Zionism's future into even greater uncertainty.

As Israel's new Kadima Party seeks a practical recipe for both peace and strength, radical Zionist ambition simmers, and the globally wired Haredi *shtetl* flexes its political muscle from Brooklyn to Jerusalem. Scholars of Jewish life and thought continue to debate what Jay Harris called the politics of fundamentalist nomenclature. The term *fundamentalism,* however, slowly gains currency in public discussions of Jewish life. Human rights activists and public intellectuals, especially in the Israeli press, warn of Jewish fundamentalism's threat to Israeli democracy and Middle East stability. Even academics who eschew the word *fundamentalism* attach a cautionary note to their otherwise objective treatments of antisecular movements in international Jewry. Ian Lustick's concern about "the seductive but perilous temptations of redemption,"[15] voiced in the wake of the 1984 Temple Mount bomb scare, still haunts virtually everyone engaged in the study of contemporary Judaism's volatile right flank.

Beyond Abrahamic Fundamentalisms

A major challenge facing the cross-confessional approach to fundamentalism is the question of fundamentalist ferment outside the triad of Western religions rooted in ancient Near Eastern

monotheism. At every stage in the development of fundamentalism studies, as we have seen throughout this narrative, the intellectual community has divided into ideological and methodological
camps over the content and usage of *fundamentalism*. Purists have
restricted the term to "angry" born-again Protestants, outraged by
modernist dissent within the community of faith and worried by
what they perceive to be secular society's assault upon Christian
values outside church walls. Comparativists have broadened the
meaning of the construct to include separatist, apocalyptic, and
antisecular movements in Catholicism, Islam, and Judaism, each
radicalized by its own experience of the crisis of modernity and
intensely engaged in its own kind of double-front culture war.

Even comparativists, however, have parted ways when the
discussion has considered fundamentalisms beyond the circle of
Abrahamic faiths. If the hypothesis of Catholic, Jewish, and Muslim fundamentalisms remains tangled in a cluster of historical,
theoretical, and methodological problems, to what extent can we
speak responsibly of fundamentalist currents in Hinduism,
Sikhism, Buddhism, and other world religions? Does the theologically and politically explosive *fundamentalism,* invented by an
American Baptist belligerent in the turbulent era after World War
I, correspond to anything in the complex worlds of South and East
Asian religions today?

Sociologist Steve Bruce has observed that religions "differ
in their potential for fundamentalist movements."[16] Many scholars agree. Some have suggested that the phenomenon of fundamentalism is uniquely related to the worldview engendered by
monotheism and its "jealous" deity. A clear trend in fundamentalism studies has been the practice of isolating monotheistic traditions, on the premise that they inherently possess greater
propensity for fundamentalist patterns of thought and behavior
than polytheistic or nontheistic systems. From classics such as
David Hume's *Natural History of Religion* (1757) and William
James's *A Pluralistic Universe* (1909) to more recent studies such
as Rodney Stark's *One True God* (2001) and *For the Glory of God*

(2003), numerous works have exposed monotheism's curious and tragic tendency to effect division as well as unity.[17] Heresy trials, witch hunts, genocidal crusades, homophobic discrimination, and racist colonialism, they maintain, have given monotheism's universal legacy an ironically exclusivist twist. Armed with such evidence, some researchers have argued that the very psychology of monotheism makes it an unusually rich breeding ground for forms of bibliolatry, creedalism, and legalism consistent with fundamentalist approaches to reality.

Other comparativists have found the reasoning behind this association of fundamentalism with monotheism to be significantly flawed. First, they say, it mistakes the accidents of some fundamentalisms (scripturalism, creedalism, and legalism) for the essence of all fundamentalisms (militant religious antimodernism). Second, it confuses the moral defects of Western monotheism with the distinctive features of fundamentalism's multilayered response to modernity — thus, smuggling a critique of fundamentalism under the guise of an objective analysis of monotheism's historical trajectory. Third, the linkage incorrectly assumes that non-Abrahamic traditions are naturally more tolerant and inclusive than their Western counterparts. Falling prey to a facile "Orientalism" that contrasts a timeless ideal of Eastern spirituality with the quotidian realities of Western faiths, the monotheism-fundamentalism theory fails to submit the religions of Asia to the same critical review that it demands for a responsible study of Western religions.

Scholars critical of the monotheism-fundamentalism correlation see believer-practitioners outside the sphere of Abrahamic faiths as at least prospective members of fundamentalism's "hypothetical family." They gather evidence for non-Abrahamic species of fundamentalisms from new faith-based protest movements proliferating in the unstable climate of postcolonial Asia. According to their analysis, these movements have reinvigorated (and reinvented) traditional cultural identity for certain populations in the face of a Western-driven globalization process perceived by mai to be the carrier of neocolonial modes of modernity laced with alien values and a "heretical imperative" inimical to ethnic enclaves and ancient worldviews. These "synthetic" or "syncretic" fundamentalisms, as some theorists have labeled them,[18] translate into vernacular terms strategies of retrenchment and innovative realignment analogous to evangelical defenses of Victorian sexual codes, Catholic reclamation of Tridentine liturgies, and Islamic calls for international jihad.

Most accounts of a Hindu fundamentalism have focused on spikes in anti-Western sentiment and interreligious friction in contemporary Indian society. Highly publicized acts of *sati* (widow burning), vandal attacks on shops selling Western-style Valentine's Day cards, enthusiastic responses to TV adaptations of ancient Hindu epics, controversial attempts to rewrite history textbooks, the murder of foreign Christian missionaries, spirals of violence swirling around sites held sacred by both Muslims and Hindus, and a series of grisly "temple wars" have led some interpreters to speak of an indigenous Indian equivalent of Western fundamentalism. Since the publication of Daniel Gold's essay on "Organized Hinduisms" in *Fundamentalisms Observed,* comparativists and South Asia scholars have begun to use *fundamentalism* to refer to an aggressive style of Hindu nationalism characterized by a self-consciously constructed sense of *Hindutva* (Hindu-ness) profoundly at odds with the set of conventional spiritual paths and philosophies traditionally associated with the term *Hinduism.*[19]

Some researchers have concentrated on patriotic and cultural organizations that situate Hindu nationalism in India's institutional life. Others have investigated the ideology of the movement, calling it an alternative to the pluralist vision articulated by M. K. ʾndhi and the secularist vision advocated by the mainstream ʾ National Congress Party. Historians have sought to reconcourse of its development, tracing its roots to the reform ʾ of the nineteenth-century neo-Hindu renaissance. ʾte 1990s, when the political arm of the nationalist movement, the Bharatiya Janata Party, dominated India's government and launched the nation's nuclear weapons program, observers spoke frankly of the triumph of fundamentalism in India.[20] The rhetoric cooled somewhat in 2004, when the Congress Party returned to power under the leadership of a moderate Sikh prime minister.

Specialists and critics alike, however, maintain that militant Hindu nationalism continues to function as a potent force in Indian culture and the international Hindu community—in populist form, in right-wing journalism, and on the Internet. New scholarly activists, calling for an "intellectual warrior class" to take up the cause of Hinduism in the "clash of civilizations," serve as intellectual gadflies in the academic establishment, challenging the integrity of mainstream Indology and questioning the "myth of the Hindu Right."[21] Today when scholars refer to Hindu fundamentalism what they have in mind is an intentionally politicized Hinduism, dedicated to any number of the following values: defense of *Sanatana Dharma* (eternal religion); promotion of premodern gender roles; protection of a precisely defined confessional identity; and confrontation with Muslim, Christian, and secular opponents.

Discussions of Sikh and Buddhist fundamentalisms have tracked similar phenomena and drawn similar conclusions. Efforts to establish Sikh home rule in the Punjab, sparked by New Delhi's push to restructure India's provincial governments and economic system in the decades following independence, contributed for many years to the everyday postcolonial chaos of the world's largest democracy. In 1984, however, when Indian troops stormed the tradition's holiest shrine and Sikh bodyguards retaliated by assassinating Prime Minister Indira Gandhi, the movement attracted international media attention. The image of a Sikh fundamentalist entered the popular imagination for the first time. Beyond what one writer has called the "violence and venality" of the horrific episode, which included a massacre of nearly three thousand innocent Sikhs, some experts have seen in the separati movement earmarks of a recognizable fundamentalist mentality. In a tradition otherwise known for its critique of caste and its affirmation of sexual equality, themes of minority consciousness, communal identity, and the merger of creed and country have invested Sikhism's symbol of the double-edged sword with new and paradoxically unmodern meanings — meanings, as Indian sociologist T. N. Madan has maintained, that intersect with concerns of classical fundamentalism.[22]

Likewise, students of recent trends in South and East Asian religious life have found some of the most prominent Buddhist movements since World War II to be motivated by fundamentalist-style antagonism toward key aspects of the modern experience. Movements reviewed have ranged from puritanical sects in Thailand to Soka Gakkai International, the humanist Buddhist lay organization of 12 million members founded in postwar Japan and best known for its peace initiatives and its aggressive proselytizing.[23] A matter of ongoing debate is whether so-called New Religious Movements — such as Aum Shinrikyo, the Hindu-Buddhist millennialist group that attacked Tokyo subways with nerve gas in 1995 — should also properly be considered as fundamentalist.

The prime candidate for a genuine Buddhist fundamentalism, according to scholarly consensus, is the Theravada nationalist movement that has contributed to the civil strife plaguing Sri Lanka for several years. A unique form of Buddhist patriotism has played a major role in ongoing conflict with Tamil separatist guerrilla fighters since the early 1980s. As Tessa Bartholomeusz and Chandra De Silva argued in *Buddhist Fundamentalism and Minority Identities in Sri Lanka* (1998), the Buddhist nationalist movement in the former colony of Ceylon, grounded in a mythic understanding of the island's world-historical destiny, has left little ˉial or conceptual space for Hindus, Muslims, or Christians in a ˡese society exclusively devoted to Buddhist *dharma* (truth). ˙ng religion as the "foundation for identity," the ˙led movement has for decades run headlong into ˙mptions of modernity such as individual autonomy, state neutrality toward religion, and the multicultural pattern of the secular social contract.[24] For Donald Swearer, director of Harvard's Center for the Study of World Religions, it is precisely this intense "quest for and assertion of identity"—after the disorienting "fall" into postcolonial modernity—that ultimately distinguishes Buddhist fundamentalisms from traditional forms of Buddhism and other new variants of the international *dharma* tradition.[25]

The Future of Comparative Fundamentalism Studies

A sober assessment of the contemporary state of academic Asian studies would indicate that the cross-cultural category of fundamentalism has exerted only minimal impact on the way that specialists in the interdisciplinary enterprise look at the phenomenon of religion. Many scholars, already wary of what Robert Cummings Neville has called "the imperialism of interpretive categories,"[26] remain profoundly suspicious of fundamentalism—both the concept and the reality. Fundamentalism has its cultured despisers in every quarter of the intellectual community. Even premier Asianists, lacking substantial knowledge of the growing body of critical literature on the topic, simply assume that fundamentalism is irrelevant to their areas of inquiry. At the same time, comparativists who utilize the analytical category of fundamentalism are often professionally locked in academic disciplines far removed from the institutional circles of formal Asian studies. Opportunities for collaboration and mutual exchange, consequently, are significantly forestalled. The much-lamented fragmentation of higher education itself, aggravated by overspecialization and politicized turf loyalties, rarely allows a concept so highly charged as fundamentalism to wander very far from its department or program of origin.

Similarly, it is safe to assume that most leaders and practitioners in the traditions of Hinduism, Sikhism, and Buddhism, particularly in the West, would flatly reject the suggestion that their traditions harbor fundamentalist elements of their own.

Some associate the idea of fundamentalism exclusively with eth-nocentric Christianity or vengeful Islam. Others may be com-pletely unaware of the varieties of antimodernist discontent transforming their tradition in other parts of the world. Some would object to the concept on dogmatic grounds, asserting that the logic of their tradition's internal belief structure renders it immune to the absolutism of fundamentalism. Lacking a culti-vated historical consciousness, some might also see their tradition as invulnerable to the vicissitudes of temporal experience arguably so essential to the generation of fundamentalisms. Eth-nic practitioners of these traditions, segregated as they often are in insular immigrant communities, may simply be incapable of thinking about their faith in terms other than those derived from its native ethos of myth and doctrine. Converts, as anecdotal evi-dence suggests, typically reserve *fundamentalism* for the reli-gions they have left behind.

Nevertheless, just as the academic study of fundamentalism has achieved a certain measure of respect in Western religious studies, it is reasonable to project the eventual acceptance of fun-damentalism as a basic interpretive tool in the study of all world religions. As we have seen throughout this survey, the study of Protestant fundamentalism matured over the course of several decades. It evolved through stages marked by Shailer Mathews's modernist appraisal, H. Richard Niebuhr's reductionist dismissal, Sandeen's and Marsden's objective analysis, and Brenda Brasher's empathetic understanding, if not guarded humanist appreciation. The fields of Catholic, Islamic, and Jewish funda-mentalism studies currently betray signs of the same sort of phased development. Scholars in these areas and leaders in the traditions themselves are earnestly struggling, while still some-times stigmatizing the phenomena they examine, to make sense of the unprecedented religious movements that have become part and parcel of what many are now calling the new world disorder. The mixture of unrest and innovation so characteristic of Asian religious life today virtually guarantees that the self-conscious methodological and theoretical sophistication presently found in Christian and Islamic fundamentalism studies will one day be standard fare in the study of non-Muslim Asian fundamentalisms.

Dialogue: The Final Frontier

The final frontier for comparative fundamentalism studies may well be full engagement with fundamentalists in interreligious dialogue. Taking this step will move comparativists into the realm of interior dialogue with the "other"—what Jesuit theologian Francis X. Clooney has called the "inscription of the self" in the comparative project.[27] A bold plea for such dialogue was greeted with enthusiasm by participants at the 1999 Parliament of the World's Religions in Cape Town. Five years later, at the Parliament meeting in Barcelona, several large sessions, including one featuring author Karen Armstrong, demonstrated that many nonfundamentalists in the international interfaith community sincerely wish to explore these uncharted waters. From their own testimonies, representatives from more traditional and conservative perspectives, previously excluded from the inner circles of dialogue, have made it clear that they are ready to open a historic new chapter in the story of interreligious exchange.[28]

In recent years, some of the world's "great souls" have begun to press toward the mark of this expanded dialogue. Pope John Paul II's unprecedented World Days of Prayer for Peace in Assisi effectively demonstrated how solidarity among religions could be promoted without surrender of principle or sacrifice of confessional identity. Former Iranian president Mohammad Khatami's call for an alternative to the "clash of civilizations" paradigm, articulated in *Hope and Challenge* (1997) and a historic speech before the UN General Assembly, dramatically sparked an ongoing conversation exploring the potential for a genuine "dialogue among civilizations."[29] England's chief rabbi Jonathan Sacks has argued eloquently for the creation of new strategies in global dialogue to boost interfaith relations to a new level. "It is religion not so much in its modern but in its counter-modern guise that has won adherents in today's world," he observed in *The Dignity of Difference* (2002), "and it is here that the struggle for tolerance, coexistence and non-violence must be fought."[30] In a special issue of *Parabola* magazine dedicated to the theme of fundamentalism, Muslim philosopher Seyyed Hossein Nasr has called the crossing of previously closed religious boundaries "the only exciting intellectual adventure of our times."[31] Pioneers in interfaith dialogue's last frontier hold the key to more than just the future state of comparative religious studies. In the age of fundamentalism, fulfillment of the Enlightenment's dream of universal toleration depends on dialogue with modernity's God-intoxicated discontents.

Epilogue

One of the most engaging single-volume experiments in comparative fundamentalism studies, treating both Western and Eastern traditions, is Niels Nielsen's *Fundamentalism, Mythos, and World Religions* (1993). It nicely sums up the accomplishments of the study of world fundamentalisms at the present time. Long associated with the study of religion at Rice University in Houston, Texas, Nielsen taught and published as a generalist. He anchored his wide-ranging research interests in a deeply abiding concern for human rights and interreligious appreciation. His major contribution to fundamentalism scholarship, drawing upon the best studies available at the time and the intuitions of a seasoned student of world religions, was the conviction that fundamentalism represents a distinctive response to "short-term as well as long-term crises of mythos." The cash value of fundamentalism, he concluded, has translated into deep-seated resistance to modernity's universal project of re-creating every aspect of human life without reference to the transcendent standard or power symbolized by myth. Above all, Nielsen was able to communicate in stark and forceful terms the sense of crisis at the core of all fundamentalisms—East and West. "For fundamentalists," he wrote, "the sacred house is on fire."[1]

For almost a hundred years, "angry" residents of the secular city have smelled smoke in the temple and sounded the midnight alarm of spiritual distress. From beleaguered Baptists to mobilized Muslims, they have come to see the modern experience not as a crucible for the purification of outworn creeds but as a raging holocaust bent on the destruction of a city "whose builder and maker is God" (Heb 11:10, KJV). Enraged by the ruin of what they deem most precious, and bracing for a final conflagration foretold by prophets, those who would "do battle royal for the fundamentals" have pledged themselves in various ways to pluck what they can from the scorching blaze and invoke divine wrath on the mortals who struck the match.

At the same time, these pilgrims in the "strange country" of modernity have rarely been content to dwell in tents. Amid the smoke and fury, rescue and recovery efforts have evolved into impressive projects of reconstruction, restoration, and outright creation. The ultimate mystery of fundamentalism—often missed by its proponents and critics alike—has been its uncanny ability to live in two worlds simultaneously. Commands directing the campaign against the "dictatorship of relativism" have issued directly from the heart of the pluralistic global village. Previews of the planet's final battle have been broadcast round the clock via satellite and the World Wide Web. Plots to destroy the materialism and militarism of godless empires have been hatched in cyber cafes and video-gambling joints. Never completely independent from their status as moderns, modernity's religious discontents have displayed a curious habit of rebuilding their cherished temples with materials confiscated from their archenemies.

The student of comparative fundamentalisms is invited today to investigate one of the most fascinating and remarkable religious movements of all time. The evidence is spread across continents and scattered throughout virtually all the world's confessions. What America's Jerry Falwell called "the religious phenomenon of the twentieth century" shows no sign of abating in the twenty-first century. Decades of critical scholarship on his extended spiritual family have yielded tremendous insights into our age—an era marked, as Schweitzer once said, by a "dangerous medley of civilization and barbarism."[2] Fundamentalism is an enduring and emblematic feature of life in the troubled modern world.

Notes

Introduction

1. Jerry Falwell (with Ed Dobson and Ed Hindson), eds., *The Fundamentalist Phenomenon: The Resurgence of Conservative Christianity* (Garden City, NY: Doubleday, 1981), 1.

2. Robert Wuthnow, *Christianity in the Twenty-first Century* (New York: Oxford University Press, 1993), 109; Gabriel A. Almond, R. Scott Appleby, and Emmanuel Sivan, *Strong Religion: The Rise of Fundamentalisms around the World* (Chicago: University of Chicago Press, 2003), 1.

3. See Philip Jenkins, *The Next Christendom: The Coming of Global Christianity* (New York: Oxford University Press, 2002).

4. Jay M. Harris, "'Fundamentalism': Objections from a Modern Jewish Historian," in *Fundamentalism and Gender,* ed. John Stratton Hawley (New York: Oxford University Press, 1994), 137–73.

5. Paul Tillich, *Systematic Theology,* 3 vols. (Chicago: University of Chicago Press, 1967), 1:86.

6. See Richard Hofstadter, *The Paranoid Style in American Politics, and Other Essays* (New York: Knopf, 1965).

7. Bruce B. Lawrence, *Defenders of God: The Fundamentalist Revolt Against the Modern Age* (Columbia: University of South Carolina Press, 1995), xii.

8. Lewis Perry, *Intellectual Life in America: A History* (New York: Franklin Watts, 1984), 263–316. See David A. Hollinger, "The

Problem of Pragmatism," *Journal of American History* 67 (June 1980): 88–107.

9. Samuel S. Hill, Jr., foreword, in *Tried as by Fire: Southern Baptists and the Religious Controversies of the 1920s,* by James J. Thompson, Jr. (Macon, GA: Mercer University Press, 1982), xv.

10. For various perspectives on the Southern Baptist controversy, see Joe Edward Barnhart, *The Southern Baptist Holy War* (Austin: Texas Monthly Press, 1986); Bill J. Leonard, *God's Last and Only Hope: The Fragmentation of the Southern Baptist Convention* (Grand Rapids, MI: Eerdmans, 1990); Walter B. Shurden and Randy Shepley, eds., *Going for the Jugular: A Documentary History of the SBC Holy War* (Macon, GA: Mercer University Press, 1996); Jerry Sutton, *The Baptist Reformation: The Conservative Resurgence in the Southern Baptist Convention* (Nashville: Broadman and Holman, 2000); Carl Kell, ed., *Voices of the Southern Baptist Convention Holy War* (Knoxville: University of Tennessee Press, 2006).

11. John Hick, *A Christian Theology of Religions* (Louisville, KY: Westminster John Knox Press, 1995), 134.

12. Harold Coward, *A Short Introduction to Pluralism in the World Religions* (Boston: Oneworld Publications, 2000), 147.

13. See Peter A. Huff, "The Challenge of Fundamentalism for Interreligious Dialogue," *Cross Currents* (Spring–Summer 2000): 94–102 and "Comparative Theology and the Future of Fundamentalism Studies," *Sewanee Theological Review* 45 (Christmas 2001): 75–83.

14. George M. Marsden, *Understanding Fundamentalism and Evangelicalism* (Grand Rapids, MI: Eerdmans, 1991), 6.

15. See Mark A. Noll, *The Rise of Evangelicalism: The Age of Edwards, Whitefield and the Wesleys* (Downers Grove, IL: InterVarsity Press, 2003); Robert H. Krapohl and Charles H. Lippy, *The Evangelicals: A Historical, Thematic, and Biographical Guide* (Westport, CT: Greenwood Press, 1999).

16. Randall Balmer, *Blessed Assurance: A History of Evangelicalism in America* (Boston: Beacon Press, 1999), 9.

17. See http://www.wheaton.edu/isae/defining_evangelicalism. html.

18. David Bebbington, "Evangelicalism in Its Settings: The British and American Movements since 1940," in *Evangelicalism,* ed. Mark A. Noll, David W. Bebbington, and George A. Rawlyk (New York:

Oxford University Press, 1994), 366. See David Bebbington, *Evangelicalism in Britain: A History from the 1730s to the 1980s* (London: Unwin Hyman, 1989), 2–17; Mark A. Noll, *American Evangelical Christianity: An Introduction* (Malden, MA: Blackwell, 2001), 12–15.

19. See Donald W. Dayton and Robert K. Johnston, eds., *The Variety of American Evangelicalism* (Knoxville: University of Tennessee Press, 1991). See also Robert E. Webber, *The Younger Evangelicals: Facing the Challenges of the New World* (Grand Rapids, MI: Baker, 2002).

20. Marshall Berman, *All That Is Solid Melts into Air: The Experience of Modernity* (New York: Penguin Books, 1988), 11.

21. Peter L. Berger, *The Heretical Imperative: Contemporary Possibilities of Religious Affirmation* (Garden City, NY: Anchor Books, 1980).

22. See T. J. Jackson Lears, *No Place of Grace: Antimodernism and the Transformation of American Culture 1880–1920* (New York: Pantheon, 1981); Peter J. Schmitt, *Back to Nature: The Arcadian Myth in Urban America* (New York: Oxford University Press, 1969).

23. Friedrich Nietzsche, *The Antichrist,* 7, in *The Portable Nietzsche,* ed. and trans. Walter Kaufmann (New York: Penguin Books, 1982), 574. See Sigmund Freud, *Civilization and Its Discontents,* trans. James Strachey (New York: W. W. Norton, 1961) and *The Future of an Illusion,* trans. James Strachey (New York: W. W. Norton, 1961).

24. Quoted in Angus Calder, *T. S. Eliot* (Atlantic Highlands, NJ: Humanities Press International, 1987), 161.

25. T. S. Eliot, *After Strange Gods: A Primer of Modern Heresy* (New York: Harcourt, Brace and Company, 1934), 65.

26. Seyyed Hossein Nasr, *Islam: Religion, History, and Civilization* (New York: HarperCollins, 2003), xv. See Mark J. Sedgwick, *Against the Modern World: Traditionalism and the Secret Intellectual History of the Twentieth Century* (New York: Oxford University Press, 2004).

Chapter One: The Evangelical Roots of Fundamentalism and Fundamentalism Studies

1. See Edwin S. Gaustad, *The Great Awakening in New England* (New York: Harper and Row, 1957); Nathan O. Hatch, *The Democratization of American Christianity* (New Haven: Yale University Press, 1989).

2. See Douglas A. Sweeney, *The American Evangelical Story: A History of the Movement* (Grand Rapids, MI: Baker, 2005); Leonard I. Sweet, ed., *The Evangelical Tradition in America* (Macon, GA: Mercer University Press, 1984).

3. Donald W. Dayton, *Discovering an Evangelical Heritage* (New York: Harper and Row, 1976).

4. See Keith J. Hardman, *Charles Grandison Finney, 1792–1875* (Syracuse, NY: Syracuse University Press, 1987).

5. See E. Brooks Holifield, *The Gentlemen Theologians: American Theology in Southern Culture 1795–1860* (Durham, NC: Duke University Press, 1978); Albert J. Raboteau, *Slave Religion: The "Invisible Institution" in the Antebellum South,* updated ed. (New York: Oxford University Press, 2004); C. C. Goen, *Broken Churches, Broken Nation: Denominational Schisms and the Coming of the American Civil War* (Macon, GA: Mercer University Press, 1985). See also John B. Boles, *The Great Revival: Beginnings of the Bible Belt* (Lexington: University Press of Kentucky, 1996); Christine Leigh Heyrman, *Southern Cross: The Beginnings of the Bible Belt* (New York: Alfred A. Knopf, 1997).

6. See Charles Reagan Wilson, *Baptized in Blood: The Religion of the Lost Cause, 1865–1920* (Athens: University of Georgia Press, 1980).

7. Samuel S. Hill, "Religion," in *Encyclopedia of Southern Culture,* ed. Charles Reagan Wilson and William Ferris (Chapel Hill: University of North Carolina Press, 1989), 1269.

8. Flannery O'Connor, *Mystery and Manners* (New York: Farrar, Straus and Giroux, 1969), 44.

9. See William M. Shea and Peter A. Huff, eds., *Knowledge and Belief in America: Enlightenment Traditions and Modern Religious Thought* (Cambridge: Cambridge University Press, 1995).

10. Perry Miller, *Jonathan Edwards* (Amherst: University of Massachusetts Press, 1981), 72, 305.

11. Henry F. May, *The Enlightenment in America* (New York: Oxford University Press, 1976).

12. See Theodore Dwight Bozeman, *Protestants in an Age of Science: The Baconian Ideal and Ante-Bellum American Religious Thought* (Chapel Hill: University of North Carolina Press, 1977).

13. Sydney E. Ahlstrom, "The Scottish Philosophy and American Theology," *Church History* 24 (September 1955): 267.

14. Mark A. Noll, *America's God: From Jonathan Edwards to Abraham Lincoln* (New York: Oxford University Press, 2002); E. Brooks Holifield, *Theology in America: Christian Thought from the Age of the Puritans to the Civil War* (New Haven: Yale University Press, 2003).

15. Timothy L. Smith, *Revivalism and Social Reform: American Protestantism on the Eve of the Civil War* (Baltimore: Johns Hopkins University Press, 1957; 1980 edition).

16. See Susan Curtis, *A Consuming Faith: The Social Gospel and Modern American Culture* (Columbia: University of Missouri Press, 2001); Timothy Miller, *Following In His Steps: A Biography of Charles M. Sheldon* (Knoxville: University of Tennessee Press, 1987).

17. Bruce J. Evensen, *God's Man for the Gilded Age: D. L. Moody and the Rise of Modern Mass Evangelism* (New York: Oxford University Press, 2003), 34.

18. See Mark A. Noll, ed., *The Princeton Theology 1812–1921: Scripture, Science, and Theological Method from Archibald Alexander to Benjamin Breckinridge Warfield* (Grand Rapids, MI: Baker, 2001).

19. William Ellery Channing, "Unitarian Christianity," in *An American Reformation: A Documentary History of Unitarian Christianity*, ed. Sydney E. Ahlstrom and Jonathan S. Carey (Middletown, CT: Wesleyan University Press, 1985), 92.

20. Quoted in Edwin S. Gaustad, *Sworn on the Altar of God: A Religious Biography of Thomas Jefferson* (Grand Rapids, MI: Eerdmans, 1996), 146.

21. Gary Dorrien, *The Making of American Liberal Theology: Imagining Progressive Religion 1805–1900* (Louisville, KY: Westminster John Knox Press, 2001). See Gary Dorrien *The Making of American Liberal Theology: Idealism, Realism, and Modernity 1900–1950*

(Louisville, KY: Westminster John Knox Press, 2003) and *The Making of American Liberal Theology: Crisis, Irony, and Postmodernity 1950–2005* (Louisville, KY: Westminster John Knox Press, 2006). See also Kenneth Cauthen, *The Impact of American Religious Liberalism* (New York: Harper and Row, 1962).

22. See Owen Chadwick, *From Bossuet to Newman: The Idea of Doctrinal Development* (Cambridge: Cambridge University Press, 1957). See also Jacques Barzun, *Darwin, Marx, Wagner: Critique of a Heritage* (Boston: Little, Brown and Company, 1941).

23. Quoted in Martin E. Marty, *Pilgrims in Their Own Land: 500 Years of Religion in America* (New York: Penguin Books, 1984), 300. See David N. Livingstone, *Darwin's Forgotten Defenders: The Encounter Between Evangelical Theology and Evolutionary Thought* (Vancouver: Regent College Publishing, 1984).

24. Bernard Lonergan, "Prolegomena to the Study of the Emerging Religious Consciousness of Our Time," in *A Third Collection: Papers by Bernard J. F. Lonergan, S.J.,* ed. Frederick E. Crowe (Mahwah, NJ: Paulist Press, 1985), 55–99.

25. Paul Carter, *The Spiritual Crisis of the Gilded Age* (DeKalb: Northern Illinois University Press, 1971).

26. Jerry Wayne Brown, *The Rise of Biblical Criticism in America, 1800–1870: The New England Scholars* (Middletown, CT: Wesleyan University Press, 1969).

27. George Tyrrell, *Tradition and the Critical Spirit: Catholic Modernist Writings,* ed. James C. Livingston (Minneapolis: Fortress Press, 1991), 127.

28. William R. Hutchison, *The Modernist Impulse in American Protestantism* (Durham, NC: Duke University Press, 1976; 1992 edition).

29. R. Scott Appleby, *"Church and Age Unite!" The Modernist Impulse in American Catholicism* (Notre Dame, IN: University of Notre Dame Press, 1992), 2.

30. Hutchison, *The Modernist Impulse,* 275.

31. Shailer Mathews, "Theology as Group Belief," in *Contemporary American Theology: Theological Autobiographies,* Second Series, ed. Vergilius Ferm (New York: Round Table Press, 1933), 163–93.

32. Tyron Inbody, "History of Empirical Theology," in *Empirical Theology: A Handbook,* ed. Randolph Crump Miller (Birmingham, AL: Religious Education Press, 1992), 11–12.

33. Shailer Mathews, *The Faith of Modernism* (New York: Macmillan, 1924), 35. Italics in original.

Chapter Two: The Birth and Rebirth
of Fundamentalism Studies

1. Many editions of *The Fundamentals* have appeared over the years—in print and on-line. The full text can be found in R. A. Torrey and A. C. Dixon, eds., *The Fundamentals: A Testimony to the Truth,* 4 vols. (Grand Rapids, MI: Baker, 2000).

2. See William Vance Trollinger, Jr., *God's Empire: William Bell Riley and Midwestern Fundamentalism* (Madison: University of Wisconsin Press, 1990).

3. John W. Bradbury, "Curtis Lee Laws and the Fundamentalist Movement," *Foundations* 5 (January 1962): 55.

4. Curtis Lee Laws, "Convention Side Lights," *The Watchman-Examiner* 8 (July 1, 1920): 834.

5. "Fundamentalism Is Very Much Alive," *The Watchman-Examiner* 9 (July 28, 1921): 941.

6. See C. Allyn Russell, *Voices of American Fundamentalism: Seven Biographical Studies* (Philadelphia: Westminster Press, 1976).

7. Shailer Mathews, *The Messianic Hope in the New Testament* (Chicago: University of Chicago Press, 1905) and *Will Christ Come Again?* (Chicago: American Institute of Sacred Literature, 1917).

8. Shirley Jackson Case, *The Millennial Hope* (Chicago: University of Chicago Press, 1918), vi, 233, 241. See "The Premillennial Menace," *Biblical World* 52 (July 1918): 16–23.

9. William Warren Sweet, *The Story of Religion in America* (New York: Harper and Brothers, 1939), 569.

10. Shailer Mathews, *The Faith of Modernism* (New York: Macmillan, 1924), 17–19 and *New Faith for Old: An Autobiography* (New York: Macmillan, 1936), 276, 287. See Shailer Mathews, "Fundamentalism and Modernism: An Interpretation," *American Review* 2 (January–February 1924): 1–9.

11. John M. Mecklin, *The Survival Value of Christianity* (New York: Harcourt, Brace, Jovanovich, 1926); Andre Siegfried, *America Comes of Age: A French Analysis* (New York: Harcourt, Brace,

Jovanovich, 1927). See James J. Thompson, Jr., *Tried as by Fire: Southern Baptists and the Religious Controversies of the 1920s* (Macon, GA: Mercer University Press, 1982), 155–56.

12. Niebuhr's famous summary of a theologically bankrupt liberalism is found in *The Kingdom of God in America* (New York: Harper and Row, 1937), 193: "A God without wrath brought men without sin into a kingdom without judgment through the ministrations of a Christ without a cross."

13. H. Richard Niebuhr, *The Social Sources of Denominationalism* (Cleveland: Meridian, 1929; 1968 edition), 184, 186.

14. Thompson, *Tried as by Fire,*156.

15. Quoted in Ernest R. Sandeen, *The Roots of Fundamentalism: British and American Millenarianism, 1800–1930* (Grand Rapids, MI: Baker, 1978), xv.

16. H. Richard Niebuhr, *The Meaning of Revelation* (New York: Macmillan, 1941), 3 and *Christ and Culture* (New York: Harper and Row, 1951; 1975 edition), 102.

17. Paul Tillich, *Systematic Theology,* 3 vols. (Chicago: University of Chicago Press, 1967), 1: 3; Reinhold Niebuhr, *Leaves from the Notebook of a Tamed Cynic* (San Francisco: Harper and Row, 1980), 162.

18. Stewart G. Cole, *The History of Fundamentalism* (Hamden, CT: Archon Books, 1931; 1963 edition), xiii.

19. Ibid., 53, 328.

20. Ibid., 38, 82, 192, 242, 328, 334.

21. Ibid., 337.

22. J. Gresham Machen, *Christianity and Liberalism* (Grand Rapids, MI: Eerdmans, 1923; 1946 edition), 165, 167.

23. See D. G. Hart, *Defending the Faith: J. Gresham Machen and the Crisis of Conservative Protestantism in Modern America* (Phillipsburg, NJ: P and R Publishing, 2003).

24. Sweet, *The Story of Religion,* 572.

25. See Robert Moats Miller, *Harry Emerson Fosdick: Preacher, Pastor, Prophet* (New York: Oxford University Press, 1985).

26. Joel A. Carpenter, *Revive Us Again: The Reawakening of American Fundamentalism* (New York: Oxford University Press, 1997).

27. William R. Glass, *Strangers in Zion: Fundamentalists in the South 1900–1950* (Macon, GA: Mercer University Press, 2001). See

B. Dwain Waldrep, "Lewis Sperry Chafer and the Development of Inter-denominational Fundamentalism in the South, 1900–1950" (PhD diss., Auburn University, 2001).

28. Albert G. Miller, "The Construction of a Black Fundamentalist Worldview," in *African Americans and the Bible: Sacred Texts and Social Textures,* ed. Vincent L. Wimbush (New York: Continuum, 2000), 721–27. See Albert G. Miller, "The Rise of African-American Evangelicalism in American Culture," in *Perspectives on American Religion and Culture,* ed. Peter W. Williams (Malden, MA: Blackwell, 1999), 259–69. See also William Hiram Bentley, *National Black Evangelical Association: Bellwether of a Movement, 1963–1988* (Chicago: National Black Evangelical Association, 1988).

29. Kenneth K. Bailey, "The Antievolution Crusade of the Nineteen-Twenties" (PhD diss., Vanderbilt University, 1953); Norman F. Furniss, *The Fundamentalist Controversy, 1918–1931* (Hamden, CT: Archon Books, 1963); Louis Gasper, *The Fundamentalist Movement* (The Hague: Mouton and Company, 1963), viii; Roland Tenus Nelson, "Fundamentalism and the Northern Baptist Convention" (PhD diss., University of Chicago Divinity School, 1964).

30. Robert T. Handy, "Fundamentalism and Modernism in Perspective," *Religion in Life* 24 (Summer 1955): 381–94; C. C. Goen, "Fundamentalism in America," *Southwest Journal of Theology* 2 (1959): 52–62.

31. Kenneth K. Bailey, *Southern White Protestantism in the Twentieth Century* (New York: Harper and Row, 1964); Willard B. Gatewood, Jr., *Preachers, Pedagogues, and Politicians: The Evolution Controversy in North Carolina, 1920–1927* (Chapel Hill: University of North Carolina Press, 1966). See William E. Ellis, "Evolution, Fundamentalism, and the Historians: An Historiographical Review," *The Historian* 44 (November 1981): 15–27.

32. See Paul K. Conkin, *When All the Gods Trembled: Darwinism, Scopes, and American Intellectuals* (Lanham, MD: Rowman & Littlefield, 1998); Edward J. Larson, *Summer for the Gods: The Scopes Trial and America's Continuing Debate over Science and Religion* (Cambridge, MA: Harvard University Press, 1997).

33. Ernest R. Sandeen, "Defining Fundamentalism: A Reply to Professor Marsden," *Christian Scholar's Review* 1 (Spring 1971): 228.

34. George Marsden, "Defining Fundamentalism," *Christian Scholar's Review* 1 (Winter 1971): 142.

35. Sandeen, "Defining Fundamentalism," 228.

36. Sandeen, *The Roots of Fundamentalism,* xv.

37. See Margaret Lamberts Bendroth, *Fundamentalists in the City: Conflict and Division in Boston's Churches, 1885–1950* (New York: Oxford University Press, 2005).

38. Sandeen, *The Roots of Fundamentalism,* 285.

39. Ernest R. Sandeen, *The Origins of Fundamentalism: Toward a Historical Interpretation* (Philadelphia: Fortress Press, 1968), 11; Francis L. Patton quoted in Sandeen, *The Roots of Fundamentalism,* 115.

40. Sandeen, *The Roots of Fundamentalism,* xxiii.

41. Norman Cohn, *The Pursuit of the Millennium,* rev. ed. (New York: Oxford University Press, 1970); Perry Miller, *Errand into the Wilderness* (Cambridge, MA: Harvard University Press, 1956), chapter 10; C. C. Goen, "Jonathan Edwards: A New Departure in Eschatology," *Church History* 28 (1959): 25–40; Ernest Lee Tuveson, *Redeemer Nation: The Idea of America's Millennial Role* (Chicago: University of Chicago Press, 1968).

42. Sandeen, *The Roots of Fundamentalism,* 42.

43. No adequate critical biography of John Nelson Darby exists. See Larry Crutchfield, *The Origins of Dispensationalism: The Darby Factor* (Lanham, MD: University Press of America, 2002).

44. See Joseph M. Canfield, *The Incredible Scofield and his Book* (Vallecito, CA: Ross House Books, 1988).

45. Timothy P. Weber, *Living in the Shadow of the Second Coming: American Premillennialism, 1875–1982,* new ed. (Chicago: University of Chicago Press, 1987). See Paul Boyer, *When Time Shall Be No More: Prophecy Belief in Modern American Culture* (Cambridge, MA: Belknap Press, 1992) and "The Growth of Fundamentalist Apocalyptic in the United States," in *The Encyclopedia of Apocalypticism,* ed. Bernard McGinn, John J. Collins, and Stephen J. Stein, 3 vols. (New York: Continuum, 2000), 3:140–78.

46. Sandeen, *The Roots of Fundamentalism,* 42.

Chapter Three: The Varieties of Protestant Fundamentalism Studies

1. See George W. Dollar, *A History of Fundamentalism in America* (Greenville, SC: Bob Jones University Press, 1973) and *The Fight for Fundamentalism: American Fundamentalism, 1973–1983* (Sarasota, FL: Daniels Publishing Company, 1983); Jerry Falwell (with Ed Dobson and Ed Hindson), eds., *The Fundamentalist Phenomenon: The Resurgence of Conservative Christianity* (Garden City, NY: Doubleday, 1981): Jim Owen, *The Hidden History of the Historic Fundamentalists, 1933–1948: Reconsidering the Historic Fundamentalists' Response to the Upheavals, Hardships, and Horrors of the 1930s and 1940s* (Lanham, MD: University Press of America, 2004).

2. David O. Beale, *In Pursuit of Purity: American Fundamentalism Since 1850* (Greenville, SC: Unusual Publications, 1986).

3. See Robert S. Ellwood, *Alternative Altars: Unconventional and Eastern Spirituality in America* (Chicago: University of Chicago Press, 1979); *The Fifties Spiritual Marketplace: American Religion in a Decade of Conflict* (New Brunswick, NJ: Rutgers University Press, 1997); and *The Sixties Spiritual Awakening: American Religion Moving from Modern to Postmodern* (New Brunswick, NJ: Rutgers University Press, 1994).

4. William G. McLoughlin, *Revivals, Awakenings, and Reform* (Chicago: University of Chicago Press, 1978).

5. Martin E. Marty, *Religion and Republic: The American Circumstance* (Boston: Beacon Press, 1987), 18.

6. See Wade Clark Roof and William McKinney, *American Mainline Religion: Its Changing Shape and Future* (New Brunswick, NJ: Rutgers University Press, 1987); William R. Hutchison, ed., *Between the Times: The Travail of the Protestant Establishment in America, 1900–1960* (Cambridge: Cambridge University Press, 1989).

7. See Diana L. Eck, *A New Religious America: How a "Christian Country" Has Become the World's Most Religiously Diverse Nation* (San Francisco: HarperSanFrancisco, 2001).

8. Roger Finke and Rodney Stark, *The Churching of America 1776–1990* (New Brunswick, NJ: Rutgers University Press, 1992), 238. See Robert Wuthnow, *The Restructuring of American Religion: Society*

and Faith Since World War II (Princeton, NJ: Princeton University Press, 1988).

9. Richard Quebedeaux, *The Young Evangelicals* (New York: Harper and Row, 1974) and *The Worldly Evangelicals* (New York: Harper and Row, 1978).

10. Quoted in Joel A. Carpenter, *Revive Us Again: The Reawakening of American Fundamentalism* (New York: Oxford University Press, 1997), 187.

11. See Cecil M. Robeck, Jr., *The Azusa Street Mission and Revival: The Birth of the Global Pentecostal Movement* (Nashville: Thomas Nelson, 2006); Estrelda Alexander, *The Women of Azusa Street* (Cleveland: Pilgrim Press, 2005).

12. Allan Anderson, *An Introduction to Pentecostalism: Global Charismatic Christianity* (Cambridge: Cambridge University Press, 2004), 155. See Robert M. Anderson, *Vision of the Disinherited: The Making of American Pentecostalism* (Peabody, MA: Hendrickson, 1979); Harvey Cox, *Fire From Heaven: The Rise of Pentecostal Spirituality and the Reshaping of Religion in the Twenty-first Century* (Cambridge, MA: Da Capo Press, 2001); Grant Wacker, *Heaven Below: Early Pentecostals and American Culture* (Cambridge, MA: Harvard University Press, 2001).

13. See William Martin, *With God on Our Side: The Rise of the Religious Right in America*, rev. ed. (New York: Broadway Books, 2005).

14. For a biographical treatment of Marsden, see Maxie B. Burch, *The Evangelical Historians: The Historiography of George Marsden, Nathan Hatch, and Mark Noll* (Lanham, MD: University Press of America, 1996).

15. Carl F. H. Henry, *The Uneasy Conscience of Modern Fundamentalism* (Grand Rapids, MI: Eerdmans, 2003), xvii, 13.

16. Edward John Carnell, *The Case for Orthodox Theology* (Philadelphia: Westminster Press, 1959), 113; Edward John Carnell, "Fundamentalism," in *A Handbook of Christian Theology*, ed. Marvin Halverson and Arthur A. Cohen (Cleveland: World, 1958), 142–43.

17. Mark A. Noll, *The Scandal of the Evangelical Mind* (Grand Rapids, MI: Eerdmans, 1994), 130. For a complementary British perspective on the evangelical assessment of fundamentalism, see J. I. Packer, *"Fundamentalism" and the Word of God* (Grand Rapids, MI: Eerdmans, 1958). For more sanguine evangelical evaluations of the fundamentalist legacy, see Richard J. Mouw, *The Smell of Sawdust: What*

Evangelicals Can Learn from Their Fundamentalist Heritage (Grand Rapids, MI: Zondervan, 2000) and Randall Balmer, *Growing Pains: Learning to Love My Father's Faith* (Grand Rapids, MI: Brazos Press, 2001).

18. George M. Marsden, *Fundamentalism and American Culture: The Shaping of Twentieth-Century Evangelicalism 1870–1925* (New York: Oxford University Press, 1980), 230.

19. George M. Marsden and Bradley J. Longfield, eds., *The Secularization of the Academy* (New York: Oxford University Press, 1992); George M. Marsden, *The Soul of the American University* (New York: Oxford University Press, 1994) and *The Outrageous Idea of Christian Scholarship* (New York: Oxford University Press, 1997).

20. George M. Marsden, *Jonathan Edwards: A Life* (New Haven: Yale University Press, 2003), 504.

21. George M. Marsden, *Reforming Fundamentalism: Fuller Seminary and the New Evangelicalism* (Grand Rapids, MI: Eerdmans, 1987) and *Understanding Fundamentalism and Evangelicalism* (Grand Rapids, MI: Eerdmans, 1991).

22. Marsden, *Fundamentalism and American Culture,* v, 5.

23. George M. Marsden, "Prof. Marsden's Concluding Remarks," *Christian Scholar's Review* 1 (Spring 1971): 232.

24. Marsden, *Fundamentalism and American Culture,* 224.

25. Ibid., 214.

26. Marsden, *Understanding Fundamentalism and Evangelicalism,* 1.

27. Clark H. Pinnock, "Defining Fundamentalism: A Response," in *The Fundamentalist Phenomenon: A View from Within; A Response from Without,* ed. Norman J. Cohen (Grand Rapids, MI: Eerdmans, 1990), 47; Karen Armstrong, *The Battle for God* (New York: Ballantine Books, 2000), 322.

28. Falwell, *The Fundamentalist Phenomenon,* vii.

29. R. Laurence Moore, *Religious Outsiders and the Making of Americans* (New York: Oxford University Press, 1986), 3–21.

30. Marsden, *Fundamentalism and American Culture,* 229–30.

31. Moore, *Religious Outsiders,* 150–72.

32. Kathleen C. Boone, *The Bible Tells Them So: The Discourse of Protestant Fundamentalism* (Albany: State University of New York Press, 1989), 12.

33. Margaret Lamberts Bendroth, *Fundamentalism and Gender, 1875 to the Present* (New Haven: Yale University Press, 1994); R. Marie Griffith, *God's Daughters: Evangelical Women and the Power of Submission* (Berkeley: University of California Press, 1997).

34. See Conrad Cherry, Betty A. DeBerg, and Amanda Porterfield, *Religion on Campus* (Chapel Hill: University of North Carolina Press, 2001).

35. Betty A. DeBerg, *Ungodly Women: Gender and the First Wave of American Fundamentalism* (Minneapolis, MN: Fortress Press, 1990), 5.

36. Ibid., 7, 12.

37. Ibid., 14.

38. Amanda Porterfield, *The Transformation of American Religion: The Story of a Late-Twentieth-Century Awakening* (New York: Oxford University Press, 2001), 226.

39. Clifford Geertz, *Islam Observed: Religious Developments in Morocco and Indonesia* (Chicago: University of Chicago Press, 1968); "Religion as a Cultural System," in *The Religious Situation: 1968,* ed. Donald R. Cutler (Boston: Beacon Press, 1968), 639–88; and "Thick Description: Toward an Interpretive Theory of Culture," in *The Interpretation of Cultures: Selected Essays* (New York: Basic Books, 1973).

40. Bruce Kuklick, "Myth and Symbol in American Studies," *American Quarterly* 24 (October 1972): 435–50.

41. Ninian Smart, *Worldviews: Crosscultural Explorations of Human Beliefs,* 3rd ed. (Upper Saddle River, NJ: Prentice Hall, 1995; 2000 edition).

42. Nancy Tatom Ammerman, *Bible Believers: Fundamentalists in the Modern World* (New Brunswick, NJ: Rutgers University Press, 1987); *Baptist Battles: Social Change and Religious Conflict in the Southern Baptist Convention* (New Brunswick, NJ: Rutgers University Press, 1990); and *Southern Baptists Observed: Multiple Perspectives on a Changing Denomination* (Knoxville: University of Tennessee Press, 1993).

43. Ellen M. Rosenberg, *The Southern Baptists: A Subculture in Transition* (Knoxville: University of Tennessee Press, 1989).

44. Susan Friend Harding, *The Book of Jerry Falwell: Fundamentalist Language and Politics* (Princeton, NJ: Princeton University Press, 2000).

45. See Brenda E. Brasher, *Give Me That Online Religion* (New Brunswick, NJ: Rutgers University Press, 2004); Brenda E. Brasher and Lee Quinby, eds., *Gender and Apocalyptic Desire* (London: Equinox Publishing, 2006).

46. Brenda E. Brasher, *Godly Women: Fundamentalism and Female Power* (New Brunswick, NJ: Rutgers University Press, 1998), 18, 182.

47. Ibid., 20.

48. Ibid., 99, 154, 167, 179–80.

49. Ibid., 68.

50. Ibid., 112.

Chapter Four: The Fundamentalist Impulse in Catholic Christianity

1. G. K. Chesterton, *All Is Grist* (London: Methuen, 1931), 53.

2. Ibid., 49.

3. Michael Williams, editor of *Commonweal* magazine, offered a fascinating perspective on these issues in *Catholicism and the Modern Mind* (New York: Dial Press, 1928). See especially chapter VIII on "Dayton, Tennessee."

4. William M. Shea, *The Lion and the Lamb: Evangelicals and Catholics in America* (Oxford: Oxford University Press, 2004), 277.

5. Walter Lippmann, *A Preface to Morals* (New York: Macmillan, 1929), 3, 34, 35; Irving Babbitt, *Democracy and Leadership* (Indianapolis, IN: Liberty Classics, 1979), 46, 211.

6. Richard Hofstadter, *Anti-Intellectualism in American Life* (New York: Vintage Books, 1963), 140–41.

7. Eugene LaVerdiere, *Fundamentalism: A Pastoral Concern* (Collegeville, MN: Liturgical Press, 1983); Patrick M. Arnold, "The Reemergence of Fundamentalism in the Catholic Church," in *The Fundamentalist Phenomenon: A View from Within; A Response from Without,* ed. Norman J. Cohen (Grand Rapids, MI: Eerdmans, 1990), 172–91.

8. Thomas F. O'Meara, *Fundamentalism: A Catholic Perspective* (New York: Paulist Press, 1990), 77.

9. Damien Kraus, "Catholic Fundamentalism: A Look at the Problem," *Living Light* 19 (September, 1982): 8–16.

10. See Patrick M. Arnold, "The Rise of Catholic Fundamentalism," *America* 56 (April 11, 1987): 297–302; John A. Coleman, "Who Are the Catholic 'Fundamentalists'?" *Commonweal* 116 (January 27, 1989): 42–47; and the articles in *New Catholic World* 228 (1985). See also Peter Hebblethwaite, "A Roman Catholic Fundamentalism," *Times Literary Supplement* (August 5–11, 1988): 866.

11. Gabriel Daly, "Catholicism and Modernity," *Journal of the American Academy of Religion* 53 (1985): 776, 794, 795.

12. William M. Shea, ed., *The Struggle Over the Past: Fundamentalism in the Modern World* (Lanham, MD: University Press of America, 1993).

13. See especially Peter Hebblethwaite, "A Fundamentalist Pope," and Hans Küng, "Against Contemporary Roman Catholic Fundamentalism," in *Fundamentalism as an Ecumenical Challenge,* ed. Hans Küng and Jürgen Moltmann (London: SCM Press, 1992), 88–96, 116–25.

14. Martin E. Marty and R. Scott Appleby, eds., *The Fundamentalism Project,* 5 vols. (Chicago: University of Chicago Press, 1991–95).

15. Timothy G. McCarthy, *The Catholic Tradition: Before and After Vatican II, 1878–1993* (Chicago: Loyola University Press, 1994), 81. See Giuseppe Alberigo and Joseph A. Komonchak, eds., *History of Vatican II,* 5 vols. (Maryknoll, NY: Orbis Books, 1996–2006).

16. John O'Malley, *Tradition and Transition: Historical Perspectives on Vatican II* (Wilmington, DE: Michael Glazier, 1989), 17.

17. Karl Rahner, "Towards a Fundamental Theological Interpretation of Vatican II," in *Vatican II: The Unfinished Agenda,* ed. Lucian Richard et al. (New York: Paulist Press, 1987), 12.

18. Catholic critiques of Vatican II and its aftermath are numerous and vary greatly in quality. Representative classics include Jacques Maritain, *The Peasant of the Garonne: An Old Layman Questions Himself About the Present Time,* trans. Michael Cuddihy and Elizabeth Hughes (New York: Holt, Rinehart and Winston, 1968); Louis Bouyer, *The Decomposition of Catholicism* (Chicago: Franciscan Herald Press, 1969); Dietrich Von Hildebrand, *Trojan Horse in the City of God* (Chicago: Franciscan Herald Press, 1967); George A. Kelly, *The Battle for the American Church* (Garden City, NY: Doubleday, 1979); and

Anne Roche Muggeridge, *The Desolate City: Revolution in the Catholic Church,* rev. ed. (San Francisco: Harper, 1990). See Peter A. Huff, *Allen Tate and the Catholic Revival* (New York: Paulist Press, 1996).

19. James Hitchcock, *The Decline and Fall of Radical Catholicism* (New York: Herder and Herder, 1971); *Catholicism and Modernity: Confrontation or Capitulation?* (New York: Seabury Press, 1979); and *The Recovery of the Sacred* (San Francisco: Ignatius Press, 1974; 1995 edition).

20. James Hitchcock, "Catholic Activist Conservatism in the United States," in *Fundamentalisms Observed,* ed. Martin E. Marty and R. Scott Appleby (Chicago: University of Chicago Press, 1991), 109, 114, 126, 127.

21. See Dean Hoge, William D. Dinges, Mary Johnson, and Juan Gonzales, Jr., *Young Adult Catholics: Religion in the Culture of Choice* (Notre Dame, IN: University of Notre Dame Press, 2001).

22. William D. Dinges, "Roman Catholic Traditionalism in the United States," in *Fundamentalisms Observed,* 99–100.

23. Marcel Lefebvre, *I Accuse the Council!* (Kansas City, MO: Angelus Press, 1976; 1998 edition), xv.

24. One of the bishops consecrated in 1988 wrote the only comprehensive life of Lefebvre currently available in English: Bernard Tissier de Mallerais, *The Biography of Marcel Lefebvre,* trans. Brian Sudlow (Kansas City, MO: Angelus Press, 2004).

25. See Mark Lowery, "Why Catholic Orthodoxy is not 'Catholic Fundamentalism,'" *New Oxford Review* 60 (September 1993): 14–19.

26. Mary Jo Weaver and R. Scott Appleby, eds., *Being Right: Conservative Catholics in America* (Bloomington: Indiana University Press, 1995); Mary Jo Weaver, ed., *What's Left? Liberal American Catholics* (Bloomington: Indiana University Press, 1999).

27. R. Scott Appleby, "Epilogue: What Difference Do They Make?" in *Being Right,* 334.

28. Mary Jo Weaver, *New Catholic Women: A Contemporary Challenge to Traditional Religious Authority* (Bloomington: Indiana University Press, 1986; 1995 edition); *Springs of Water in a Dry Land: Spiritual Survival for Catholic Women Today* (Boston: Beacon Press, 1993); and *Cloister and Community: Life within a Carmelite Monastery* (Bloomington: Indiana University Press, 2002).

29. R. Scott Appleby, *The Ambivalence of the Sacred: Religion, Violence, and Reconciliation* (Lanham, MD: Rowman & Littlefield, 2000).

30. James Hitchcock, "The Fellowship of Catholic Scholars: Bowing Out of the New Class," in *Being Right,* 199.

31. George Weigel, "The Neoconservative Difference: A Proposal for the Renewal of Church and Society," in *Being Right,* 140.

32. Mary Jo Weaver, "Self-Consciously Countercultural: Alternative Catholic Colleges," in *Being Right,* 319.

33. Michael W. Cuneo, "Life Battles: The Rise of Catholic Militancy within the American Pro-Life Movement," in *Being Right,* 295.

34. In addition to Appleby's contributions to the Fundamentalism Project, see "The Fundamentalism of the Enclave: Catholic and Protestant Oppositional Movements in the United States," in *New Dimensions in American Religious History,* ed. Jay P. Dolan and James P. Wind (Grand Rapids, MI: Eerdmans, 1993), 231–60. See also R. Scott Appleby, ed., *Spokesmen for the Despised: Fundamentalist Leaders of the Middle East* (Chicago: University of Chicago Press, 1997).

35. Mary Jo Weaver, "A Church We Long For: The Fundamentalist Challenge," in *The Struggle Over the Past,* 281; and "Catholic Fundamentalism," in *Encyclopedia of Fundamentalism,* ed. Brenda E. Brasher (New York: Routledge, 2001), 90.

36. Michael W. Cuneo, *Catholics Against the Church: Anti-Abortion Protest in Toronto 1969–1985* (Toronto: University of Toronto Press, 1989); *American Exorcism: Expelling Demons in the Land of Plenty* (New York: Broadway Books, 2001); and *Almost Midnight: An American Story of Murder and Redemption* (New York: Broadway Books, 2004).

37. Michael W. Cuneo, *The Smoke of Satan: Conservative and Traditionalist Dissent in Contemporary American Catholicism* (New York: Oxford University Press, 1997), 6.

38. Ibid., 40, 61 ff.

39. Ibid., 25–26, 38, 79, 87, 147.

40. Ibid., 180.

41. Jacques Maritain, *Reflections on America* (New York: Charles Scribner's Sons, 1958), 93.

42. Cuneo, *Catholics Against the Church,* 186, 197–98.

43. Cuneo, *The Smoke of Satan,* 182.

44. Quoted in George Weigel, *God's Choice: Pope Benedict XVI and the Future of the Catholic Church* (New York: HarperCollins, 2005), 140. See Joseph Ratzinger, *Truth and Tolerance: Christian Belief and World Religions,* trans. Henry Taylor (San Francisco: Ignatius Press, 2004), 120–21, 190–91.

Chapter Five: Comparative Fundamentalism Studies: Islam

1. Steve Brouwer, Paul Gifford, and Susan D. Rose, *Exporting the American Gospel: Global Christian Fundamentalism* (New York: Routledge, 1996), 1, 2, 151.

2. George M. Marsden, *Fundamentalism and American Culture: The Shaping of Twentieth-Century Evangelicalism 1870–1925* (New York: Oxford University Press, 1980), 227–28.

3. See Karl Jaspers, *The Origin and Goal of History,* trans. Michael Bullock (New Haven: Yale University Press, 1953). For a contemporary restatement of the axial age thesis, see Karen Armstrong, *The Great Transformation: The Beginning of Our Religious Traditions* (New York: Knopf, 2006).

4. Clifford Geertz, *Islam Observed: Religious Developments in Morocco and Indonesia* (Chicago: University of Chicago Press, 1968), 1.

5. Robin Wright, *Sacred Rage: The Wrath of Militant Islam* (New York: Simon and Schuster, 1986), 19.

6. R. Scott Appleby, *Religious Fundamentalisms and Global Conflict* (New York: Foreign Policy Association, 1994), 4.

7. Bruce B. Lawrence, *Defenders of God: The Fundamentalist Revolt Against the Modern Age* (Columbia: University of South Carolina Press, 1989; 1995 edition), xxv.

8. Lionel Caplan, ed., *Studies in Religious Fundamentalism* (Albany: State University of New York Press, 1987); Martin Riesebrodt, *Pious Passion: The Emergence of Modern Fundamentalism in the United States and Iran,* trans. Don Reneau (Berkeley: University of California Press, 1993); Gilles Kepel, *The Revenge of God: The Resurgence of Islam, Christianity and Judaism in the Modern World,* trans. Alan Braley (University Park: Pennsylvania State University Press, 1994); Niels C. Nielsen, Jr., *Fundamentalism, Mythos, and World Religions* (Albany: State University of New York Press, 1993).

9. Lawrence, *Defenders of God,* xx.

10. Ibid., 96, 101. See Marshall G. S. Hodgson, *The Venture of Islam: Conscience and History in a World Civilization,* 3 vols. (Chicago: University of Chicago Press, 1974), 3:176–222.

11. Lawrence, *Defenders of God,* 100–101. Italics in original.

12. Roger W. Stump, *Boundaries of Faith: Geographical Perspectives on Religious Fundamentalism* (Lanham, MD: Rowman & Littlefield, 2000); Steve Bruce, *Fundamentalism* (Cambridge: Polity Press, 2000); Richard T. Antoun, *Understanding Fundamentalism: Christian, Islamic, and Jewish Movements* (Walnut Creek, CA: AltaMira Press, 2001); Karen Armstrong, *The Battle for God* (New York: Ballantine Books, 2000); Malise Ruthven, *Fundamentalism: The Search for Meaning* (New York: Oxford University Press, 2004).

13. Martin E. Marty and R. Scott Appleby, eds., *The Fundamentalism Project,* 5 vols. (Chicago: University of Chicago Press, 1991–95).

14. Martin E. Marty and R. Scott Appleby, *The Glory and the Power: The Fundamentalist Challenge to the Modern World* (Boston: Beacon Press, 1992).

15. Gabriel A. Almond, R. Scott Appleby, and Emmanuel Sivan, *Strong Religion: The Rise of Fundamentalisms around the World* (Chicago: University of Chicago Press, 2003), 16–17.

16. Ludwig Wittgenstein, *Philosophical Investigations,* trans. G. E. M. Anscombe (New York: Macmillan, 1953), I, par. 66.

17. Ibid., I, par. 66.

18. Ibid., I, par. 67.

19. Almond, Appleby, and Sivan, *Strong Religion,* 17. Italics in original.

20. Martin E. Marty and R. Scott Appleby, eds., *Fundamentalisms Observed* (Chicago: University of Chicago Press, 1991), 835.

21. Martin E. Marty and R. Scott Appleby, eds., *Fundamentalisms Comprehended* (Chicago: University of Chicago Press, 1995), 7. Italics in original.

22. Reader Bullard, *Two Kings in Arabia: Letters from Jeddah 1923–5 and 1936–9,* ed. E. C. Hodgkin (Reading: Ithaca Press, 1993), 167–68. Malise Ruthven discovered this reference. See his *Fundamentalism,* 26–27.

23. H. A. R. Gibb, *Mohammedanism: An Historical Survey,* 2nd ed. (New York: Oxford University Press, 1962), 176.

24. R. Stephen Humphreys, "Islam and Political Values in Saudia Arabia, Egypt, and Syria," in *Religion and Politics in the Middle East,* ed. Michael Curtis (Boulder, CO: Westview Press, 1981), 289.

25. See Lawrence Davidson, *Islamic Fundamentalism: An Introduction,* rev. ed. (Westport, CT: Greenwood Press, 2003), 16–17; Abdel Salam Sidahmed and Anoushiravan Ehteshami, introduction, in *Islamic Fundamentalism,* ed. Abdel Salam Sidahmed and Anoushiravan Ehteshami (Boulder, CO: Westview Press, 1996), 4–5; Ervand Abrahamian, *Khomeinism: Essays on the Islamic Republic* (London: I. B. Tauris, 1993), 13; Ruthven, *Fundamentalism,* 28–29.

26. Akbar S. Ahmed, *Islam Today* (New York: I. B. Tauris, 1999), 226.

27. Haideh Moghissi, *Feminism and Islamic Fundamentalism: The Limits of Postmodern Analysis* (London: Zed Books, 1999), 65.

28. Roxanne L. Euben, *Enemy in the Mirror: Islamic Fundamentalism and the Limits of Modern Rationalism* (Princeton, NJ: Princeton University Press, 1999), 17; Abrahamian, *Khomeinism,* 13.

29. John L. Esposito, *The Islamic Threat: Myth or Reality?* 3rd ed. (New York: Oxford University Press, 1999), 5; Johannes J. G. Jansen, *The Dual Nature of Islamic Fundamentalism* (Ithaca, NY: Cornell University Press, 1997), 14; Seyyed Hossein Nasr, *The Heart of Islam: Enduring Values for Humanity* (New York: HarperCollins, 2002), 107.

30. Esposito, *The Islamic Threat,* 21.

31. Yvonne Yazbeck Haddad, John Obert Voll, and John L. Esposito, with Kathleen Moore and David Sawan, *The Contemporary Islamic Revival: A Critical Survey and Bibliography* (New York: Greenwood Press, 1991); Yvonne Yazbeck Haddad and John L. Esposito, with Elizabeth Hiel and Hibba Abugideiri, *The Islamic Revival Since 1988: A Critical Survey and Bibliography* (Westport, CT: Greenwood Press, 1997).

32. John L. Esposito, *Islam: The Straight Path,* rev. 3rd ed. (New York: Oxford University Press, 2005), 158, 165.

33. Esposito, *The Islamic Threat,* 5–22 and *Islam,* 166. See John L. Esposito, *Unholy War: Terror in the Name of Islam* (New York: Oxford University Press, 2002).

34. Fazlur Rahman, *Revival and Reform in Islam: A Study of Islamic Fundamentalism,* ed. Ebrahim Moosa (Oxford: Oneworld,

2000). See Fazlur Rahman, *Islam and Modernity: Transformation of an Intellectual Tradition* (Chicago: University of Chicago Press, 1982).

35. See John O. Voll, *Islam: Continuity and Change in the Modern World,* 2nd ed. (Syracuse, NY: Syracuse University Press, 1994).

36. John O. Voll, "Renewal and Reform in Islamic History: *Tajdid* and *Islah,*" in *Voices of Resurgent Islam,* ed. John L. Esposito (New York: Oxford University Press, 1983), 32–47.

37. Davidson, *Islamic Fundamentalism,* 21, 104.

38. See Ali Rahnema, ed., *Pioneers of Islamic Revival,* updated ed. (London: Zed Books, 2005); Timothy R. Furnish, "Islamic Fundamentalism," in *Encyclopedia of Fundamentalism,* ed. Brenda E. Brasher (New York: Routledge, 2001), 235–40.

39. Quoted in Paul J. Griffiths, ed., *Christianity Through Non-Christian Eyes* (Maryknoll, NY: Orbis Books, 1990), 74.

40. Quoted in Yvonne Y. Haddad, "Sayyid Qutb: Ideologue of Islamic Revival," in *Voices of Resurgent Islam,* 81, 83. See Sayyid Qutb, *Milestones* (Cedar Rapids, IA: Mother Mosque Foundation, n.d.).

41. Gilles Kepel, *Muslim Extremism in Egypt: The Prophet and Pharaoh,* trans. Jon Rothschild (Berkeley: University of California Press, 1993), 37 and *Jihad: The Trail of Political Islam,* trans. Anthony F. Roberts (Cambridge, MA: Belknap Press, 2002), 314.

42. See Samuel P. Huntington, *The Clash of Civilizations and the Remaking of World Order* (New York: Simon and Schuster, 1996).

43. See Bassam Tibi, *The Challenge of Fundamentalism: Political Islam and the New World Disorder,* updated ed. (Berkeley: University of California Press, 2002), xiii–xxiii.

44. Tariq Ali, *The Clash of Fundamentalisms: Crusades, Jihads and Modernity* (New York: Verso, 2003), xiii.

45. See Bernard Lewis, "The Roots of Muslim Rage," *The Atlantic Monthly* 266 (September 1990): 47–60.

46. Yossef Bodansky, *Bin Laden: The Man Who Declared War on America* (New York: Forum, 2001), 156.

Chapter Six: Comparative Fundamentalism Studies: Judaism and Asian Religions

1. Jonathan Webber, "Rethinking Fundamentalism: The Readjustment of Jewish Society in the Modern World," in *Studies in Religious Fundamentalism,* ed. Lionel Caplan (Albany: State University of New York Press, 1987), 119; Jacob Neusner, "What is the Challenge of Contemporary Jewish Fundamentalism?" in *Fundamentalism as an Ecumenical Challenge,* ed. Hans Küng and Jürgen Moltmann (London: SCM Press, 1992), 49.

2. Jay M. Harris, "'Fundamentalism': Objections from a Modern Jewish Historian," in *Fundamentalism and Gender,* ed. John Stratton Hawley (New York: Oxford University Press, 1994), 137–73.

3. Gideon Aran, "Jewish Zionist Fundamentalism: The Bloc of the Faithful in Israel (Gush Emunim)," in *Fundamentalisms Observed,* ed. Martin E. Marty and R. Scott Appleby (Chicago: University of Chicago Press, 1991), 333.

4. Laurence J. Silberstein, ed., *Jewish Fundamentalism in Comparative Perspective: Religion, Ideology, and the Crisis of Modernity* (New York: New York University Press, 1993).

5. Samuel Heilman, *Defenders of the Faith: Inside Ultra-Orthodox Jewry* (Berkeley: University of California Press, 2000); David Landau, *Piety and Power: The World of Jewish Fundamentalism* (New York: Hill and Wang, 1993).

6. See Peter A. Huff, "Haredim," in *Encyclopedia of Fundamentalism,* ed. Brenda E. Brasher (New York: Routledge, 2001), 207–8.

7. Landau, *Piety and Power,* 51.

8. See Aviezer Ravitzky, *Messianism, Zionism, and Jewish Religious Radicalism,* trans. Michael Swirsky and Jonathan Chipman (Chicago: University of Chicago Press, 1996) and Israel Shahak and Norton Mezvinsky, *Jewish Fundamentalism in Israel,* new ed. (London: Pluto Press, 2004).

9. Jacob Neusner, *The Way of Torah,* 3rd ed. (Belmont, CA: Wadsworth, 1979), 117.

10. David Newman, ed., *The Impact of Gush Emunim: Politics and Settlement in the West Bank* (New York: St. Martin's Press, 1985); Ehud Sprinzak, *Gush Emunim: The Politics of Zionist Fundamentalism in Israel* (New York: American Jewish Committee, 1986); Ian Lustick,

For the Land and the Lord: Jewish Fundamentalism in Israel (New York: Council on Foreign Relations, 1988).

11. Aran, "Jewish Zionist Fundamentalism," in *Fundamentalisms Observed,* 305.

12. Ibid., 295, 306. Gilles Kepel, *The Revenge of God: The Resurgence of Islam, Christianity and Judaism in the Modern World,* trans. Alan Braley (University Park: Pennsylvania State University Press, 1994), 140.

13. Gershom Gorenberg, *The End of Days: Fundamentalism and the Struggle for the Temple Mount* (New York: Oxford University Press, 2000), 208.

14. Timothy P. Weber, *On the Road to Armageddon: How Evangelicals Became Israel's Best Friend* (Grand Rapids, MI: Baker, 2004).

15. Lustick, *For the Land,* 184.

16. Steve Bruce, *Fundamentalism* (Cambridge: Polity Press, 2000), 95.

17. See Rodney Stark, *One True God: Historical Consequences of Monotheism* (Princeton: Princeton University Press, 2001) and *For the Glory of God: How Monotheism Led to Reformations, Science, Witch-Hunts, and the End of Slavery* (Princeton, NJ: Princeton University Press, 2003).

18. Gabriel A. Almond, R. Scott Appleby, and Emmanuel Sivan, *Strong Religion: The Rise of Fundamentalisms around the World* (Chicago: University of Chicago Press, 2003), 16, 90.

19. See Daniel Gold, "Organized Hinduisms: From Vedic Truth to Hindu Nation," in *Fundamentalisms Observed,* 531–93. See also Mary Ann Lind, "Hinduism, Fundamental," in *Encyclopedia of Fundamentalism,* 222–25.

20. See Christophe Jaffrelot, *The Hindu Nationalist Movement in India* (New York: Columbia University Press, 1996).

21. See David Frawley (Vamadeva Shastri), *Hinduism and the Clash of Civilizations* (New Delhi: Voice of India, 2001).

22. Patwant Singh, *The Sikhs* (New York: Doubleday, 1999), 199–242; T. N. Madan, "The Double-edged Sword: Fundamentalism and the Sikh Religious Tradition," in *Fundamentalisms Observed,* 594–627. See T. N. Madan, *Modern Myths, Locked Minds: Secularism and Fundamentalism in India* (New York: Oxford University Press, 1998).

23. See Richard Hughes Seager, *Encountering the Dharma: Daisaku Ikeda, Soka Gakkai, and the Globalization of Buddhist Humanism* (Berkeley: University of California Press, 2006).

24. Tessa J. Bartholomeusz and Chandra R. De Silva, *Buddhist Fundamentalism and Minority Identities in Sri Lanka* (Albany: State University of New York Press, 1998), 2.

25. Donald K. Swearer, "Fundamentalistic Movements in Theravada Buddhism," in *Fundamentalisms Observed,* 678.

26. Robert Cummings Neville, Preface, in *The Human Condition: A Volume in the Comparative Religious Ideas Project,* ed. Robert Cummings Neville (Albany: State University of New York Press, 2001), xv.

27. Francis X. Clooney, "Comparative Theology: A Review of Recent Books," *Theological Studies* 56 (1995): 523.

28. Elliot Miller, "Ambitious Goals, Ambiguous Results: The World's Religions Gather in Cape Town," *Christian Research Journal* 22 (2000): 6–10; Doug LeBlanc, "Parliament Focuses on Social Justice, Interfaith Cooperation," *Christian Research Journal* 27 (2004): 41–42.

29. Mohammad Khatami, *Hope and Challenge: The Iranian President Speaks,* ed. Parviz Morewedge and Kent P. Jackson, trans. Alidad Mafinezam (Binghamton, NY: Institute of Global Cultural Studies, 1997). See A. Kamal Aboulmagd, Lourdes Arizpe, et al., *Crossing the Divide: Dialogue Among Civilizations* (South Orange, NJ: Seton Hall University Press, 2001).

30. Jonathan Sacks, *The Dignity of Difference: How to Avoid the Clash of Civilizations* (London: Continuum, 2005), 18. I am indebted to Captain Herb Melendy, USN, Ret., for drawing my attention to this passage.

31. "The Sacred World of the Other: An Interview with Seyyed Hossein Nasr," *Parabola* 30 (Winter 2005): 40.

Epilogue

1. Niels C. Nielsen, Jr., *Fundamentalism, Mythos, and World Religions* (Albany: State University of New York Press, 1993), 8, 67.

2. Albert Schweitzer, *The Philosophy of Civilization,* trans. C. T. Campion (New York: Macmillan, 1950), 21.

Suggested Reading

Evangelicalism in America

Blumhofer, Edith L., and Joel A. Carpenter. *Twentieth Century Evangelicalism: A Guide to the Sources*. New York: Garland, 1990.

Dayton, Donald W., and Robert K. Johnston, eds. *The Variety of American Evangelicalism*. Knoxville: University of Tennessee Press, 1991.

Hunter, James Davison. *American Evangelicalism: Conservative Religion and the Quandary of Modernity*. New Brunswick, NJ: Rutgers University Press, 1983.

Krapohl, Robert H., and Charles H. Lippy. *The Evangelicals: A Historical, Thematic, and Biographical Guide*. Westport, CT: Greenwood Press, 1999.

Noll, Mark A. *American Evangelical Christianity: An Introduction*. Oxford: Blackwell, 2001.

Sweeney, Douglas A. *The American Evangelical Story: A History of the Movement*. Grand Rapids, MI: Baker, 2005.

Szasz, Ferenc M. *The Divided Mind of Protestant America, 1880–1930*. Tuscaloosa: University of Alabama Press, 2002.

Protestant Fundamentalism in America

Beale, David O. *In Pursuit of Purity: American Fundamentalism Since 1850*. Greenville, SC: Unusual Publications, 1986.

Brasher, Brenda E. *Godly Women: Fundamentalism and Female Power.* New Brunswick, NJ: Rutgers University Press, 1998.

Carpenter, Joel A. *Revive Us Again: The Reawakening of American Fundamentalism.* New York: Oxford University Press, 1997.

DeBerg, Betty A. *Ungodly Women: Gender and the First Wave of American Fundamentalism.* Minneapolis, MN: Fortress Press, 1990.

Harris, Harriet A. *Fundamentalism and Evangelicals.* Oxford: Clarendon Press, 1998.

Marsden, George M. *Fundamentalism and American Culture.* 2nd ed. New York: Oxford University Press, 2006.

Martin, William. *With God on Our Side: The Rise of the Religious Right in America.* Rev. ed. New York: Broadway Books, 2005.

Sandeen, Ernest R. *The Roots of Fundamentalism: British and American Millenarianism, 1800–1930.* Grand Rapids, MI: Baker, 1978.

Weber, Timothy P. *Living in the Shadow of the Second Coming: American Premillennialism, 1875–1982.* New ed. Chicago: University of Chicago Press, 1987.

Catholic Fundamentalism

Appleby, R. Scott. "The Fundamentalism of the Enclave: Catholic and Protestant Oppositional Movements in the United States." In *New Dimensions in American Religious History.* Ed. Jay P. Dolan and James P. Wind. Grand Rapids, MI: Eerdmans, 1993. 231–60.

Cuneo, Michael W. *The Smoke of Satan: Conservative and Traditionalist Dissent in Contemporary American Catholicism.* New York: Oxford University Press, 1997.

Daly, Gabriel. "Catholicism and Modernity." *Journal of the American Academy of Religion* 53 (1985): 773–96.

Weaver, Mary Jo, and R. Scott Appleby, eds. *Being Right: Conservative Catholics in America.* Bloomington: Indiana University Press, 1995.

Islamic Fundamentalism

Davidson, Lawrence. *Islamic Fundamentalism: An Introduction.* Rev. ed. Westport, CT: Greenwood Press, 2003.

Esposito, John L. *The Islamic Threat: Myth or Reality?* 3rd ed. New York: Oxford University Press, 1999.

——— , ed. *Voices of Resurgent Islam.* New York: Oxford University Press, 1983.

Euben, Roxanne L. *Enemy in the Mirror: Islamic Fundamentalism and the Limits of Modern Rationalism.* Princeton, NJ: Princeton University Press, 1999.

Haddad, Yvonne Yazbeck, and John L. Esposito, with Elizabeth Hiel and Hibba Abugideiri. *The Islamic Revival Since 1988: A Critical Survey and Bibliography.* Westport, CT: Greenwood Press, 1997.

Jansen, Johannes J. G. *The Dual Nature of Islamic Fundamentalism.* Ithaca, NY: Cornell University Press, 1997.

Kepel, Gilles. *Jihad: The Trail of Political Islam.* Trans. Anthony F. Roberts. Cambridge, MA: Belknap Press, 2002.

Milton-Edwards, Beverley. *Islamic Fundamentalism since 1945.* New York: Routledge, 2005.

Tibi, Bassam. *The Challenge of Fundamentalism: Political Islam and the New World Disorder.* Updated ed. Berkeley: University of California Press, 2002.

Voll, John O. *Islam: Continuity and Change in the Modern World.* 2nd ed. Syracuse, NY: Syracuse University Press, 1994.

Jewish Fundamentalism

Heilman, Samuel. *Defenders of the Faith: Inside Ultra-Orthodox Jewry.* Berkeley: University of California Press, 2000.

Landau, David. *Piety and Power: The World of Jewish Fundamentalism.* New York: Hill and Wang, 1993.

Lustick, Ian S. *For the Land and the Lord: Jewish Fundamentalism in Israel.* New York: Council on Foreign Relations Press, 1988.

Ravitzky, Aviezer. *Messianism, Zionism, and Jewish Religious Radicalism.* Trans. Michael Swirsky and Jonathan Chipman. Chicago: University of Chicago Press, 1996.

Shahak, Israel, and Norton Mezvinsky. *Jewish Fundamentalism in Israel.* New ed. London: Pluto Press, 2004.

Silberstein, Laurence J., ed. *Jewish Fundamentalism in Comparative Perspective: Religion, Ideology, and the Crisis of Modernity*. New York: New York University Press, 1993.

Fundamentalism in South and East Asian Traditions

Bartholomeusz, Tessa J., and Chandra R. De Silva. *Buddhist Fundamentalism and Minority Identities in Sri Lanka*. Albany: State University of New York Press, 1998.
Jaffrelot, Christophe. *The Hindu Nationalist Movement in India*. New York: Columbia University Press, 1996.
Mandan, T. N. *Modern Myths, Locked Minds: Secularism and Fundamentalism in India*. New York: Oxford University Press, 1998.

Comparative Fundamentalism Studies

Almond, Gabriel A., R. Scott Appleby, and Emmanuel Sivan. *Strong Religion: The Rise of Fundamentalisms around the World*. Chicago: University of Chicago Press, 2003.
Antoun, Richard T. *Understanding Fundamentalism: Christian, Islamic, and Jewish Movements*. Walnut Creek, CA: AltaMira Press, 2001.
Armstrong, Karen. *The Battle for God*. New York: Ballantine Books, 2000.
Brasher, Brenda E., ed. *Encyclopedia of Fundamentalism*. New York: Routledge, 2001.
Bruce, Steve. *Fundamentalism*. Cambridge: Polity Press, 2000.
Caplan, Lionel, ed. *Studies in Religious Fundamentalism*. Albany: State University of New York Press, 1987.
Hawley, John Stratton, ed. *Fundamentalism and Gender*. New York: Oxford University Press, 1994.
Kepel, Gilles. *The Revenge of God: The Resurgence of Islam, Christianity and Judaism in the Modern World*. Trans. Alan Braley. University Park: Pennsylvania State University Press, 1994.
Lawrence, Bruce B. *Defenders of God: The Fundamentalist Revolt Against the Modern Age*. Columbia: University of South Carolina Press, 1995.

Marty, Martin E., and R. Scott Appleby, eds. *The Fundamentalism Project*. 5 vols. Chicago: University of Chicago Press, 1991–95.

Nielsen, Niels C., Jr. *Fundamentalism, Mythos, and World Religions*. Albany: State University of New York Press, 1993.

Riesebrodt, Martin. *Pious Passion: The Emergence of Modern Fundamentalism in the United States and Iran*. Trans. Don Reneau. Berkeley: University of California Press, 1993.

Ruthven, Malise. *Fundamentalism: The Search for Meaning*. New York: Oxford University Press, 2004.

Shea, William M., ed. *The Struggle Over the Past: Fundamentalism in the Modern World*. Lanham, MD: University Press of America, 1993.

Stump, Roger W. *Boundaries of Faith: Geographical Perspectives on Religious Fundamentalism*. Lanham, MD: Rowman & Littlefield, 2000.

Index